Brian Sutton-Smith, Playful Scholar

Brian Sutton-Smith, Playful Scholar

A Centennial Celebration

VOLUME 17

Edited by

Michael M. Patte
Fraser Brown
Anna Beresin

HAMILTON BOOKS
AN IMPRINT OF
ROWMAN & LITTLEFIELD
Lanham • Boulder • New York • London

Published by Hamilton Books
An imprint of The Rowman & Littlefield Publishing Group, Inc.
4501 Forbes Boulevard, Suite 200, Lanham, Maryland 20706
www.rowman.com

86-90 Paul Street, London EC2A 4NE, United Kingdom

British Library Cataloguing in Publication Information Available

Library of Congress Cataloging-in-Publication Data

Names: Patte, Michael M., editor. | Brown, Fraser, 1951- editor. | Beresin, Anna
    R., editor.
Title: Brian Sutton-Smith, playful scholar : a centennial celebration / edited by Michael
    M. Patte, Fraser Brown, Anna Beresin.
Description: Lanham : Hamilton Books, an imprint of Rowman & Littlefield, [2024]
    | Includes bibliographical references and index. | Summary: "This book honors the
    legacy of Dr. Brian Sutton-Smith, Professor Emeritus of Psychology and Folklore at
    the University of Pennsylvania. We present an eclectic array of essays written in honor
    of the centennial of his birth, ranging from the scholarly to the overtly playful"—
    Provided by publisher.
Identifiers: LCCN 2024005778 (print) | LCCN 2024005779 (ebook) | ISBN
    9780761874027 (paperback) | ISBN 9780761874461 (epub)
Subjects: LCSH: Sutton-Smith, Brian. | Child psychology. | Play. | Folklore. |
    Psychologists—United States—Biography. | Folklorists—United States—Biography.
Classification: LCC BF109.S84 B75 2024 (print) | LCC BF109.S84 (ebook) | DDC
    150.92 [B]—dc23/eng/20240315
LC record available at https://lccn.loc.gov/2024005778
LC ebook record available at https://lccn.loc.gov/2024005779

For Brian, and all who play with big ideas

Contents

Figures and Tables

Foreword

James E. Johnson

Brian Sutton-Smith wrote:

> *Since I first began reflecting on the nature of play and games in 1942, I have authored or coauthored, edited, or coedited fifty or so books on these subjects. And during those sixty-five (and some) years, I thought time and again I had at last discovered the meaning of play. But somehow it always turned out otherwise; somehow there always seemed other questions to ask, other lines of inquiry to follow, all auguring answers more promising than those I thought I had in hand.*

> *Play begins as a major feature of mammalian evolution and remains as a major method of becoming reconciled with our being within our present universe. In this respect, play resembles both sex and religion, two other forms—however temporary or durable—of human salvation in our earthly box.*

The above quotes are the first and last paragraphs of an article/chapter (in the inaugural volume/issue of *American Journal of Play* (2008) and reprinted in *The Handbook of the Study of Play, vol. 1) (2015)* written by the man to whom this volume of *Play & Culture Studies* is dedicated in honor of the centennial of his birth. The volume co-editors have done us a great service bringing together a rich and varied collection of items—from empirical studies, letters, a play in three acts, to notes and snapshots and so forth—to remember our playful friend, Brian Sutton-Smith.

Brian's capstone books—*The Ambiguity of Play* (1997) and *Play for Life: Play Theory and Play as Emotional Survival* (2016)—mark his career's project, and support the widely accepted claim that Brian was and is the leading play scholar of the 20th century going into the 21st century. A playful friend, he is also our teacher, a tireless and inspirational leader. Some of us have referred to him as our guru, others as the play philosopher's philosopher. Even Play Pope!

Many of us remember Brian from the meetings of The Association for the Study of Play (TASP), originally TAASP with the extra A standing for Anthropological, because originally and in the 1970s and 1980s anthropologists were into play before play was in vogue. Still, the group was transdisciplinary, life-span, and multicultural, ahead of its times as was Brian. He was and is unique in many ways; his *fabula* (spirit of play) was second to none. He meant so much to us.

For me it started in 1975 when I saw him for the first time standing at the back of the room where I was presenting data from my dissertation at the Midwestern Psychological Association's annual conference held in Chicago. He came up after and introduced himself, and I immediately felt the electricity, his interest in my work and in me just starting off. Many can say this—it was the beginning of a beautiful relationship.

Brian cared about the field, and he cared about relationships. You will see this in the pages that follow. Enjoy the diverse items in this volume and always cherish your thoughts about Brian Sutton-Smith and his superb play scholarship.

Introduction

Michael M. Patte

2023 marks the 50th birthday of The Association for the Anthropological Study of Play (TAASP), now The Association for the Study of Play (TASP), as the first organizational meeting was held in 1973 at the American Association for Health, Physical Education, and Recreation Convention in Minneapolis under the direction of Professor Alyce Cheska. At this meeting research papers were offered, ideas were exchanged, and plans for formalizing TAASP were made. In 1974, the second meeting took place at the University of Windsor in Ontario, where Professor Michael Salter took office as the first president of TAASP. The first formal conference took place on April 3–5, 1975, in Detroit, Michigan, and was jointly sponsored by TAASP, the American Ethnological Society, and the Central States Anthropological Society. At this gathering the constitution was approved, and a governing body was elected.

For the past 50 years, TAASP/TASP remains the premier professional association in academia advancing, stimulating, and encouraging the study of play; supporting and cooperating with local, national, and international organizations having the same purpose; organizing and arranging meetings; and issuing a variety of scholarly publications concerning the purpose of the association. TAASP/TASP has generated an impressive catalogue of research publications from 1974 to present day including: edited collections of conference proceedings (1976–1987); the Play & Culture Studies series (1998-present); and three peer-reviewed journals *Play and Culture* (1988–1992), *Journal of Play Theory & Research* (1992–1997), and *The International Journal of Play* (2012-present).

The seventeenth volume of *Play and Culture Studies* celebrates the centennial of the birth of Brian Sutton-Smith in 1924, preeminent scholar of developmental psychology, children's folklore, and play. Brian's professional career spanned six decades, and his body of scholarship included the publication of 40 books and 300 articles across the alphabet of disciplines which has and will continue to inspire both students and scholars for generations. Since his death in 2015, the coeditors planned to dedicate a volume in honor of Brian's strong commitment to TASP over the years as evidenced by his presidency in 1983 and his many keynote addresses spanning some 40 years (1976, 1995, 1997, 2000, and 2004).

In her keynote address at the 40th TASP Conference in 2014 titled *Spirited Play*, former TASP president and self-proclaimed empress of play, Ann Marie Guilmette summarized Brian's seminal impact on the study of play:

> Sutton-Smith's contributions comprehensively and with precision address the scholarly nature in our studies of play. If not for his insights which are pervasive and persistent, some 40 years later we would still be limited, ignored, and rejected as a "fringe" endeavor. Early on, Brian's work was dismissed as "too edgy" with his emphasis on cruel play, vulgar play, or dark play. Brian has been bold and brave in his studies of emotions and aesthetics (or the arts). Society dictates that valuable research would be focused on the study of cognition, of knowledge and/or facts such as those pursuits in the math and the sciences. Sutton-Smith has been the brave, the bold, the visionary, and the ultimate player. Brian has known the struggles, been subjected to the ridicule, risen to the challenges, and yet he has persisted. When TASPians have faltered in the last 40 years, we have called upon Sutton-Smith, and he has not disappointed us. Rather his efforts have emboldened and emblazoned us. Otherwise, we might still be condemned as outcasts, who chase immature, unimportant pursuits that are not worthwhile. As play researchers we would still be chided and chastised as outsiders in the sacred grove.

> Like play, those who would study such a topic would otherwise be doomed to be castigated and relegated to the hinterland, where we would have been discarded, sacrificed, dismissed, isolated, ignored, and excluded. The spirits and the spirited Sutton-Smith convince us that we are real scientists. Consistent with the required principles, our studies in play can certainly be considered as scholarship. Thanks to our 40 years of persistence and dedication, we can be highly regarded for adhering to and advancing an orderly, systematic, substantive, and rigorous understanding and interpretation of play that would be expected of any scientific inquiry.

We are conscious that Brian was not only a ground-breaking thinker, but also a very playful person. The Editors made a deliberate effort to reflect that in the content of this volume. The contributions to the seventeenth volume of *Play and Culture Studies* are eclectic in nature and come from Brian Sutton-Smith's contemporaries, students, colleagues, friends, and those inspired by his life's work. Brian's legacy lives on.

Chapter 1

An Ever-Incomplete Conversation Between Three Books

Homo Ludens *by Johan Huizinga* The Ambiguity of Play *by Brian Sutton-Smith* The Ecology of Imagination in Childhood *by Edith Cobb*

Sylwyn Guilbaud

When, long ago, I was a playwork student, I would walk along the shelves of the university library, listening to the books as my fingertips ran along the spines. In this way I discovered many authors in many unlikely sections, which I would otherwise never have found. I was always very interested by the books on either side of those which I heard most clearly. This, not incidentally, was how I first came across Brian Sutton-Smith's writing, in *The Masks of Play* co-authored with Diana Kelly-Byrne—misplaced, having wandered from play into another adjoining area.

These days I have my own library of books about play and other subjects, I do not have an organised system of classification, which means I forget what I have, and re-find fascination when I go looking for a title. I still pay attention to the books that have ended up next to the one that I was looking for; and more than that, when I am working with an idea, reflecting or getting ready to write, I sometimes ask the books to help by piling them in a stack so that they can talk to each other, so that when I open them I might overhear new ways of understanding.

When I received the email call for contributions for this special celebration of Brian Sutton- Smith, I went looking for *The Ambiguity of Play*, and found it in a pile, with *Homo Ludens* by Johan Huizinga underneath and *The Ecology of Imagination in Childhood* by Edith Cobb, on top. And so, I wondered if I might be able to write and contribute something in the form of a conversation between these three books. This would not be an academic critique, and could of course not be anywhere near a comprehensive reflections of these deep, un-exhaustible texts; but rather, I hope, it might be an expression of my experience of listening for the conversation between them. I was not, and in this morning of tentative beginning, am still not, sure exactly how to write this, what approach or voice to take which will convey this, but I am imagining the conversation will create its own form.

But how? How to communicate something which is so personal, which I know only from the shell that it happens, or from the inside as it happens. Is there any value, might there be dis-value? When considering writing this I spoke to my long-time friend and mentor Professor Fraser Brown, who was also a good friend of Brian Sutton-Smith. He shared with me a story of being left in Brian's personal library one evening and of his exploration of so many books, which had so many notes in the margins, wonderful reflections between the text and other writings or thoughts. Fraser told me that Brian loved connections between things, but had no time for the wishy washy. As the disquiet rises in me I consider our human inclination towards abstraction, and the potential dangers which Gregory Bateson, and now his daughter Nora, identify in this way that the mind works—to wit, that meaning might be made from too little information (Bateson, N. 2023).

These books are big, they are significant, they are life's contributions, there is too much, and I am wasting words on this uncomfortable questioning, this was a foolish idea. And yet, this has never once been a consideration before, when it is just me listening to the rustles between the pages, imagining, trusting, not watching myself. Is this not something worth communicating to others, especially new scholars of play, that there is value in playfully finding out, that there is joy in learning incidentally rather than deliberately, that there might be value in the liminal page margins of possibility.

Perhaps I can ease myself in, can I make a frame out of the frame? I begin unusually for me, with the introduction of *The Ambiguity of Play*: 'Almost everything can allow play to occur within its boundaries' (p.3). I feel again the complex layers of Sutton-Smith's careful, yes full of care, years of honed attention, his palpable fascination with play in the way he creates the frame, the rhetorics; his putting next to each other of that which is not play, but that through which play is unavoidably contextualised, approached, presented, used, contained. In these first pages I feel the lightness of his way through his specific-ness and also with the shining through of playfulness, his own humanness, humour. All these rhetorics of life, which seem heavy somehow in their obscuring lens, are by this sorting of vast studies of play to be used themselves to illuminate the light of our firefly, play—I feel as if I have never read this book before.

I feel the slight slip of play within my being, a lightness too at the outskirts of my head, a kind of sensory metamorphosis of my perception of liminality, then a stuttering as I try to split myself a little so that I can trace this process. I notice what I am bringing from within, to meet this introduction of *ambiguity*. A little responsive singsong refrain *Play, play with thoughts about play, take the solid, the real about the not real, the respected, that which can be used by others to see play, and remake it soft, play.* With the thought of softening,

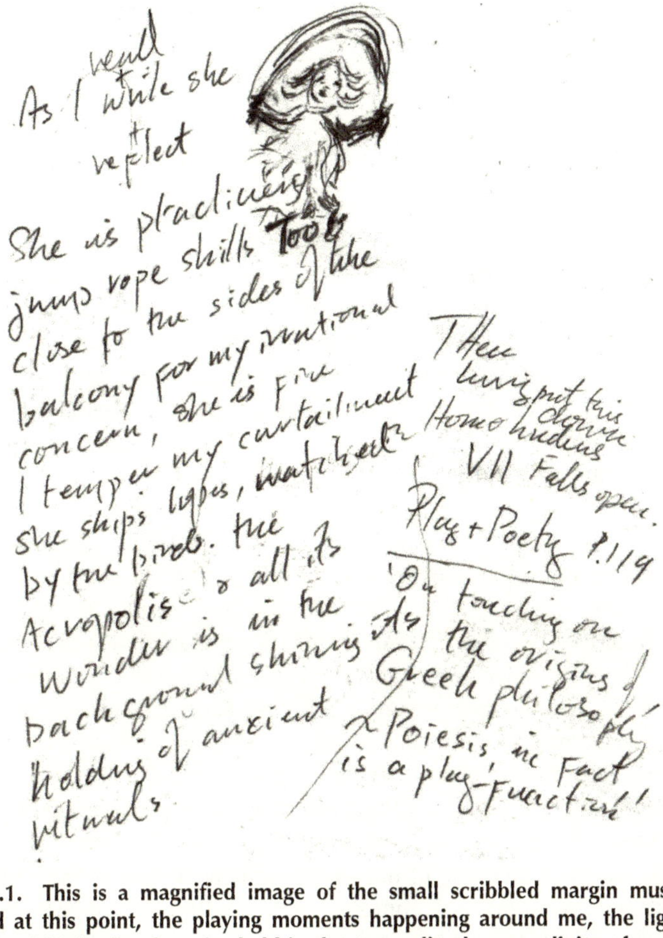

Figure 1.1. This is a magnified image of the small scribbled margin musings that appeared at this point, the playing moments happening around me, the lightness of skipping and birds, the rhetorics held in the Acropolis, the serendipity of pages falling open in Homo Ludens.

or unravelling the *real* or reified, my interpretation and repeated probing of Gadamer's discussion of how play becomes real (Gadamer, Weinsheimer & Marshall 2004; Gadamer as discussed in Guilbaud 2011, 2018, 2021) mixes with my comfort blanket corner of Borh's discussion of the way in which the essence of life disappears when we try to dissect something living to find it (Borh 1956; Borh discussed in Guilbaud 2011, 2018, 2021).

And so, I open *The Ecology of Imagination in Childhood*, at a page with a bent corner and at the top of the left hand page there is this:

> We ought, therefore, to be able to cast off the shackles of a super-intellectualism as total technique without abandoning logic at the level of the gestalt. We can then turn our observation of the homespun beauty of the child's thoughts and play, the child's perceptual worlds, to better use without muddying the water of adult speculation. (Cobb p.24)

This paragraph sooths me, it gives me a sense of ground for my thoughts about frame, but then I wonder if perhaps it is too obvious, that it might seem untrue, contrived that I happened to find it here? My body shrugs, this is playing, it cannot be what it is not, for then it will be nothing, so I can only trust that you the reader can trust in my integrity, that this which I am sharing with you is true, as it happens.

From this paragraph I read backwards to Cobb's writing about Klee, who she reads as having written about love of nature as 'unitary action' with love of knowledge 'mind and body interacting with the universe' (p.22) and I read forward to the bottom of page 25 where she describes her own journey.

So imagine imagination, I am playing at imagining this playful conversing—I open *The Ambiguity of Play* again, just open the book and read; what is this about, this page does not touch me; but wait, stay, female non-contest, I tuck this page into the description of Cobb's journey and leave them on the sofa. I take a pause, that the pages may mingle themselves, and that the listening space in my mind may grow from this possibility to make room, and then I dip back.

In the final two pages of *Prelude to a Method* Cobb notes the unfortunate language of conquest which still maintains a supreme hold on 'our social and political theory, our medical policies, and most serious of all, our teaching of ideas about nature and man' (p.24). Yet in this page spread, she carries us, through her faith in the web of life and our readiness for this way of knowing, to the description of her own process of research. 'The recognition of the value of true metaphor would seem to be the key to the journey, leading as it does to the ultimate meaning of human transcendence and to the understanding of our most precious tool, compassionate intelligence' (p.25).

These pages were tucked between pages 102 and 103 of *The Ambiguity of Play*, where Sutton-Smith discusses identity and festivals. He writes 'some feminist literature seeks to use play as pleasure, as against play as contest, as a statement of desirable female identity. In the 1980s, some declared women's essential being to lie in play.' Those open pages of *The Ecology of Imagination in Childhood*, of Edith Cobb's life work, of her disappointment in the language of contest, reach into this through me, *yes*. Then in the last paragraph of p.103 there is the back and forth stepping of yes and no, the light human touch that recurs throughout *The Ambiguity of Play*, ambiguity itself.

'Lest these various advocacies seem a little strange, I should mention that they are very much in tune with the experience of many children, particularly girls, who find that the most important thing about play is to be included and not excluded from the group's activities.' (p.103)

I'm not so sure about this generalisation, generalisations are tricky, there is uneasiness in this paragraph for me, connection and generalisation, community and identity, beauty and diminishment somehow, yes ambiguity.

I turn over p.104, eyes slide to the bottom of p.105, the subtitle *The Independent Cultures of Play*, over to p.106 'Play is about the ontology of being a player and the dreams that that sustains. It is only indirectly about the epistemology of creating other forms of competence.'

And here this conversation between pages starts to become more, thinner fly away paper, mille-feuille patterning into the periphery of my awareness, the subject of connection, the process overlap, the play of metaphor in all the metaphor of play, jumps of thoughts that through their relationship and their difference reflect more, play distilled and removed but through its resonance re-creatable, re-playable, I am writing without thinking now, the decaying leaf that once fluttered will again and then I've gone too far, that possibility of perception disappears.

And from this a question:

Is play always intruded upon, is that life, what would it be if it were not?

Homo Ludens, wake up!

Huizinga's first paragraph echoes the affect of its companions here; there is breadth, or beauty or something meaningful. I love the contents of this book, and I remember all the times I have used it. I return to read the part about words for play. I remember the first time I read this. I add a little something that I heard yesterday about the Russian language having different words for light and dark blue and how the brain of those who speak Russian lights up differently in response to those colours—here we are again then, the unavoidability of the context, this is not new, its everywhere, but it is important to have awe for it all, is it not?

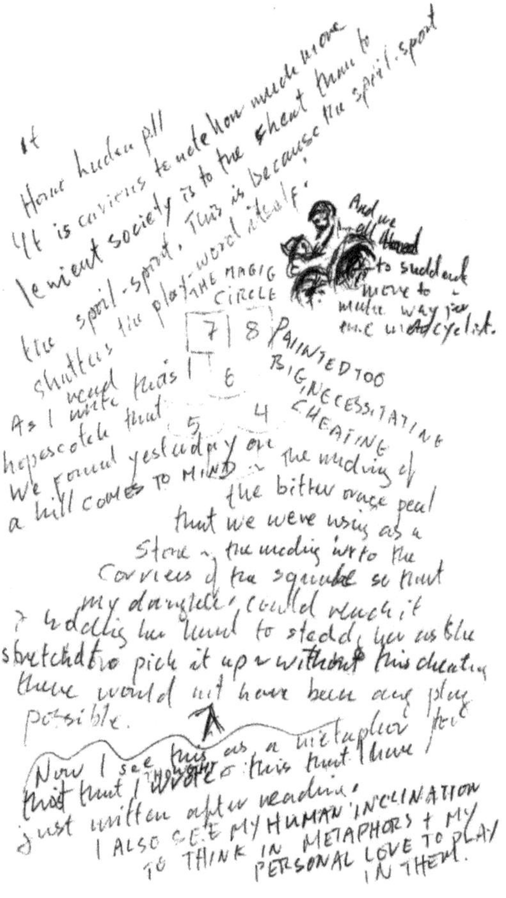

Figure 1.2. This is a note from a scrap of paper reflecting the fun of coming across an oversized hopscotch drawn on a hill, and playing with orange skin instead of a stone. As my pencil drew this happenstance I became aware of metaphoric relevance; the motorbike spoilsport, the flexible collaborative cheating/re-ruling to reach into the corner of the too big frame, and my human inclination to understand play-fully in metaphor, all reflecting the conversations between the book pages I had been dwelling with.

And then I trip, I cheat, I use the index, what does Sutton-Smith say of Huizinga. It isn't cheating, it is the next step, the thing that I wanted to do, in this game with no rules that I am making up, but it feels a bit like cheating, or that it might look like cheating,

Still . . .

'Nobody has claimed so much for play before or since, nor has anyone had as much effect on humanistic play scholars in the twentieth century' (p.202). But then the opposite page unpicks Huizinga's idealization and sanctification of play, as an act of removal from the every-day. The paragraph ends

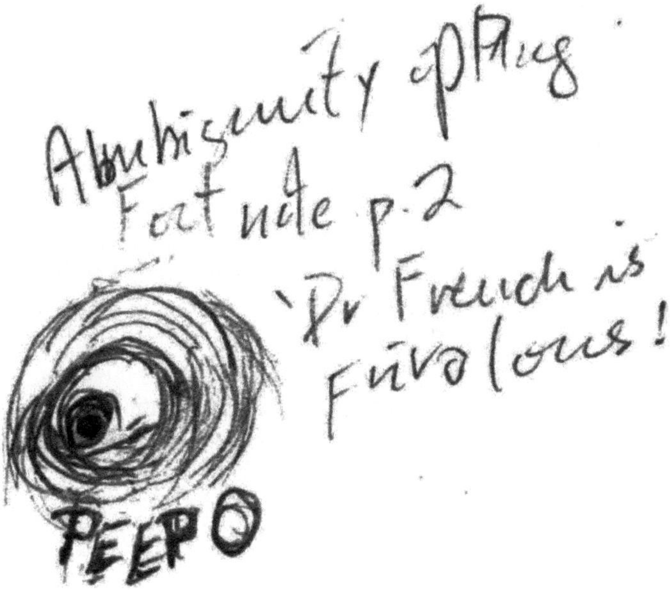

Figure 1.3. This much magnified doodle grew from a tiny dot on the corner of a page, becoming a circular knot as I struggled with the sense of diminishment of these three books, and then found restorative playfulness peeping out.

with a recognition of Huizinga's contribution to 'play's intellectual evolution from being despised to being idealized (being a) dialectical step on the way to a more adequate synthesis' (p.203). But now Homo Ludens shrinks, as it sits here in these pages, written by Sutton-Smith, classified by Huizinga's disposition, inclination, time, life experience. Then I see that *The Ecology of Imaginations in Childhood* must also fit, slot, be limited in its *ALL* and *BIG* wonder by this classification—all is smaller.

But then I flip back a page, to the first page of this chapter, *The Rhetoric of Frivolity*, and read the two snippets at the top, with which all these chapters begin; what is it that Brian wrote about them? Here I find a play-filled peep-hole.

'Don't be afraid of talking nonsense, but you must pay attention to your nonsense' Ludwig Wittgenstein

And

'Play is fun
Sex is fun.
Jokes are fun.

Writing is fun.
Being funny is fun.
So what is fun?

after Mrs Huizinga'

I laugh

Everything grows again! Imagine doing so much within our limits, imagine striving to understand play despite its *slippery malleability* (Guilbaud 2011). Imagine, within the limits that situational context imposes even on great minds, to be trying to protect play's way, to honour it.

As it is time to bring this ever-incomplete conversation to a close, I turn deliberately to these book's own closings. These great texts, these great life

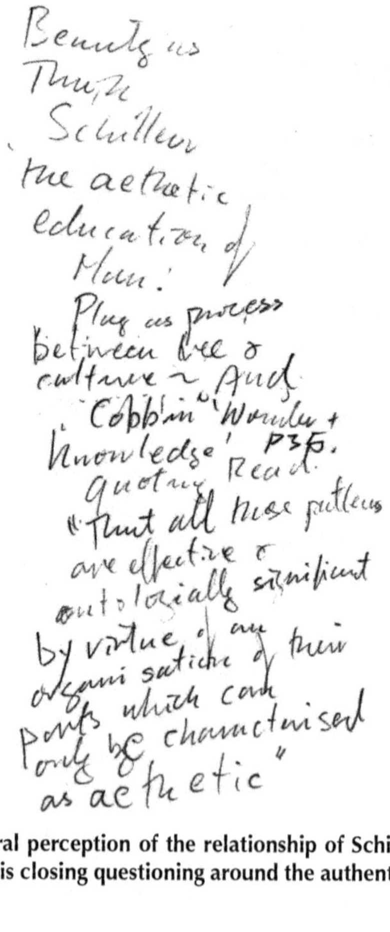

Figure 1.4. A peripheral perception of the relationship of Schiller's 'On the Aesthetic Education of Man' to this closing questioning around the authenticity of playful patterning and truth/evolving.

works that have touched so many, spurred so many, have all at the end tried to offer something conclusive enough. But even in their last pages, the beauty is not in curtain call, it is in the dance, in the tentative, in the expression of play's undoing of the self, of the thinker, of the theorists, of the researcher. In attempting to understand we are meant to be undone, are we not?

Together in their final chapters these texts illuminate such complexity of undoing in stepping forward. Firstly, in this afternoon of book opening (and in chronology of publication), Huizinga's summations in *The Play-Element in Contemporary Civilization* bear the tone of disassociation and disillusionment. Beginning with a question 'To what extent does the civilization we live in still develop in play-forms?' (p.195), lamenting the 'false play' of modern times, and closing through the sense of returning all that had been held apart for examination to the age-old proposition of play as the fulcrum of everything. Yet within the last paragraph offering our logic, our ethic, our inclination towards good, to stand in the way of the unravelling of life by play. The kernel of this steadfastness being in our capacity for pity.

Had it not been for this particular play-full conversation between three books, I might never have noticed the reflections between the last chapter of *Homo Ludens* and that of *The Ecology of Imagination in Childhood*. Now, leafing through these pages, one and then the other and then the other, there is so much refraction, in each author's considerations, and in the subject matter: truth, falseness, culture, nature, creativity, the extrapolations of child's play into the vastness of existence. Quite fascinatingly to me, Cobb's final paragraph also rests on the human capacity for tenderness. Yet in her closing, this potential for 'compassionate intelligence,' rather than being a composite of logic holding our minds from spiralling away into play, comes from the 'common-plus-cosmic' beginnings of the child's world-making in play;

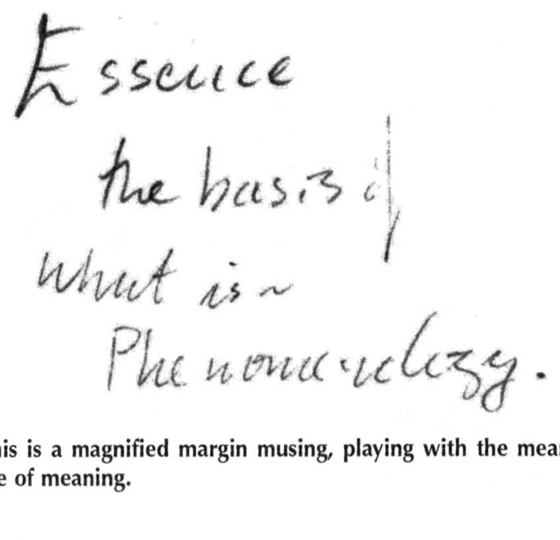

Figure 1.5. **This is a magnified margin musing, playing with the meaning of essence and the essence of meaning.**

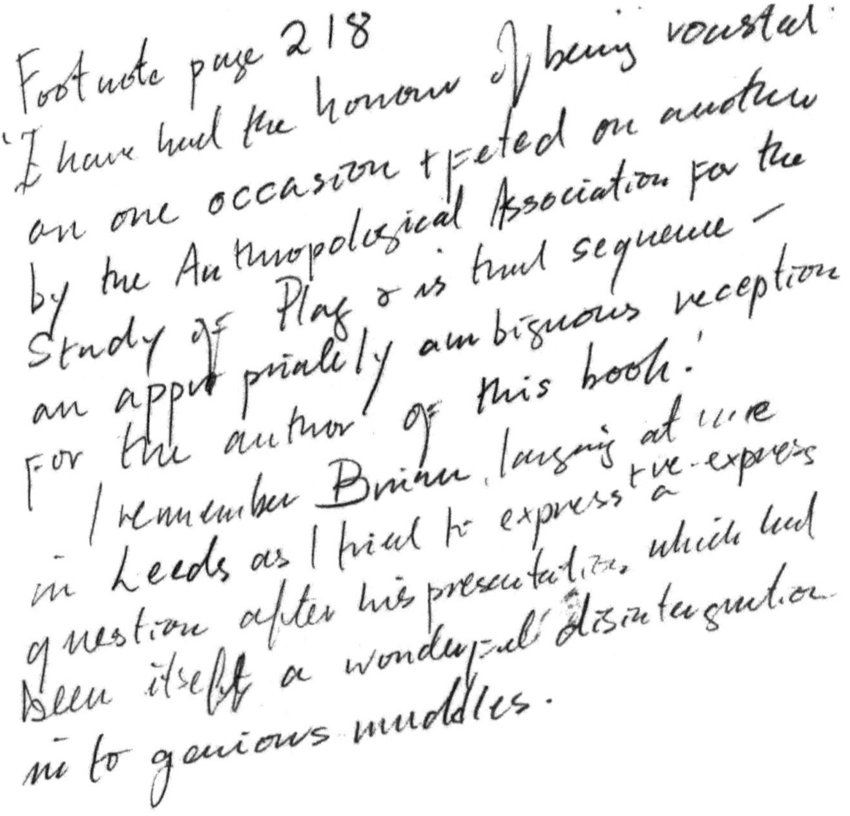

Figure 1.6.   An extra little extrapolation of Brian Sutton-Smith's fun-making, remembering my young earnestness and his merriment, long ago in a different celebration of play.

allowing for the potential which Cobb at her time of writing, saw as being ripe, that of creating creative evolution.

'Either mastery or further chaos' (p.231). These words jump out from the last paragraph of *The Ambiguity of Play*; out of context, but also not so. Selected by my eyes, my mind, due to the sensitization of the companion text's final paragraphs, yet also of essence.

Perhaps it is not so extraordinary that there should be echo between these chapters, they are after all written by those who hold play in high regard, and who have supposedly begun their comprehension of play by playing, and recognised play in myriad situations via this initial first experience-gained-understanding. Such extraordinariness is perhaps further diminished when the subject is play, for which commonality of perception lies in recognition of potentially infinite variability. In his concluding, Sutton-Smith—adding to Huizinga's tone of stating and Cobb's way of forward drawing—brings a quality of unpicking and poking fun, largely at himself, as with irony he

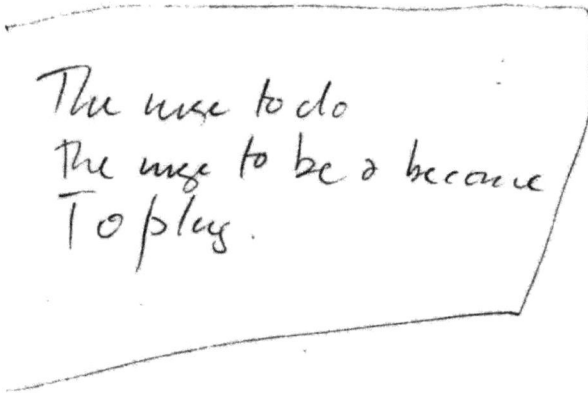

Figure 1.7. A small representation of the culminating musings around the unanswerable question of play's relationship with existence.

offers, perhaps unavoidably for the human play theorist, his view of play in our endless-changing-becoming.

As for me, perhaps I cannot help the inclination either, to offer something in closing, an inconclusive recurrent wondering arising from and dissolving into these pages, and life:

'Is play always a metaphor of itself?'

REFERENCES

Bateson, N. (2023) *Bateson Anniversaries talks 'Abductive Process'* live zoom meeting, hosted by Nora Bateson, 13th April 2023. Stockholm: The International Bateson Institute.

Bohr, N. (1958) Light and life. *Atomic physics and human knowledge.* New York: John Wiley & Sons. pp.3–8.

Cobb, E. (1993) *The ecology of imagination in childhood,* Connecticut: Spring Publications Inc.

Gadamer, H. G., Weinsheimer, J. & Marshall, D. G. (2004) *Truth and method.* London: Continuum.

Guilbaud, S. (2011) *A phenomenological inquiry into the possibility of played-with-ness in experiences with things.* Doctor of Philosophy, Leeds Metropolitan University.

Guilbaud, S. (2018) The might of play as possiblity and power, *In*: Brown, F. & Hughes, B. (eds.). *Aspects of playwork, play & culture studies, volume 14.* London: Hamilton Books. pp.107–121.

Guilbaud, S. (2021) The Ness of being playful, *In*: Jennings, S. & Holmwood, C. (eds.) *Routledge international handbook of play, therapeutic play and play therapy.* London: Routledge. pp.51–59.

Huizinga, J. (1955) *Homo ludens,* Boston: The Beacon Press.

Sutton-Smith, B. (1997) *The Ambiguity of Play,* London: Harvard University Press.

Chapter 2

Memories of Brian

A Fellow Contrarian

Gordon M. Burghardt

Brian Sutton Smith was one of my most influential mentors, although I did not actually meet him until rather late in my career, over a decade after I began writing on conceptual issues concerning animal play. This meeting was at the TASP/ICCP World Play Conference held in Salzburg, Austria in 1995. I remember listening to his fascinating presentation. I talked about animal play and showed data that seemed to be the first filmed documentation of play in a non-avian reptile, a large, and ancient, Nile Soft-Shell Turtle, named Pigface, who was on exhibit at the National Zoo in Washington, DC. Brian was interested in such a distantly non-human example of play.

At that time, I had long known of Brian's work. We both had chapters in Peter K. Smith's 1984 edited book, *Play in Animals and Humans*. We bookended the volume. I had the opening chapter, On the Origins of Play, and Brian and Diana Kelly-Byrne had the last chapter, The Idealization of Play. Their early critical analysis of the *play ethos* shaped my thinking that all proposed functions of play were poorly supported and that play was a mishmash of phenomena that needed careful critical attention, from definition to its evolutionary origins. The functions of such a heterogeneous set of phenomena could span from being multiple and diverse to non-existent. The opening of my chapter was a section titled "To Define Rainbows and Hunt for Pots of Gold" (Burghardt, 1984: 5). Sutton-Smith and Kelly-Byrne's opening sentences were: "The aim of the present chapter is to demonstrate, albeit historically and anecdotally, that what currently passes for the science of play is culturally relative. It is an ideology of play rather than a scientific theory of play" (Sutton-Smith & Kelly-Byrne, 1984: 305).

Many years later, in 1998, I wrote to him about the parallel nature of these chapters and how they encouraged and mutually confirmed my then rather heretical approach to play in animals and his skepticism about panglossian views about play in humans. Thus, our mutual dissatisfaction with play research, although derived from areas as disparate as my origins in ethology and physiology, and Brian's in education, children's games, and folklore, made us collegial sounding boards and correspondents from after the meeting in Salzburg to shortly before his last trying years.

What I remember most about Brian, from our extensive correspondence that began in 1997, and occasional contacts at play conferences, was his enthusiasm and cheerfulness about all things play, even if he never forgot the dark underbelly of play. This spanned from at least the 1984 chapter to his posthumous *Play for Life* volume (Sutton-Smith, 2017). We primarily interchanged views on our writings, and he was most helpful and encouraging. We exchanged and commented on each other's papers and chapters through regular mail and email. We particularly reflected on emotions and play, his dissatisfaction with documentaries on play, and how play was neglected or dismissed by so many prominent thinkers, otherwise viewed as seminal.

His important book, *The Ambiguity of Play* (Sutton-Smith, 1997), was the most seminal volume since Huizinga, and the seven rhetorics of play a truly groundbreaking classification. Indeed, these rhetorics were the backbone of the first chapter in my book, *The Genesis of Animal Play: Testing the Limits* that came out in 2005 after an 18-year gestation (Burghardt, 2005). In fact, perhaps the greatest debt I owe him is his writing the Foreword to my book (Sutton-Smith, 2005). It stands out to me as a significant memento of our interactions, certainly more meaningful for me than for Brian. In any event, I count him as one of the most influential persons in my scholarly playful life, as well as the most eminent play scholar of our time.

REFERENCES

Burghardt, G. M. (1984). On the Origins of Play. In *Play in Animals and Humans* (P. K. Smith, ed.). Basil Blackwell, London; pp. 5–41.

Burghardt, G. M. (2005). *The Genesis of Animal Play: Testing the Limits*. MIT Press, Cambridge, MA.

Sutton-Smith, B. (1997). *The Ambiguity of Play*. Harvard University Press, Cambridge, MA.

Sutton-Smith, B. (2005). Foreword. In G. M. Burghardt, *The Genesis of Animal Play: Testing the Limits*, pp. ix–x.

Sutton-Smith, B. (2017). *Play for Life: Play Theory and Play as Emotional Survival*. The Strong, Rochester, NY.

Sutton-Smith, B. & Kelly-Byrne, D. (1984). The Idealization of Play. In *Play in Animals and Humans* (P. K. Smith, ed.). Basil Blackwell, London, UK, pp. 305–321.

Chapter 3

Brian Sutton-Smith and the Obscurity of Play

Peter D. McDonald

Abstract: Brian Sutton-Smith's landmark text *The Ambiguity of Play* (1997) emerged after a long period of wrestling with epistemological, methodological, and disciplinary questions about play. This essay reconstructs those questions and how they inform his rhetorical approach, arguing that they show obscurities within play that cannot be explained only as the result of diverse disciplinary theories. It looks closely at how Sutton-Smith develops three sources of diversity—practices, players, and disciplines—that each point out a different type of problem within play.

Brian Sutton-Smith is justly famous for writing *The Ambiguity of Play* (1997), a work that summarizes his lifetime of wrestling with the meaning of play and its protean variation. There, Sutton-Smith foregoes a direct theorization of play and instead characterizes seven 'rhetorics' that shape discourse about it. These include the belief that play must contribute to human progress, that play is how we understand uncertainty, that play mediates group conflicts and identity, that play is at the root of creativity and imagination, and that play is caught up in enlightenment conceptions of individualism (Sutton-Smith, 1997). The diversity, mutual incompatibility, and dialectical nature of these rhetorics eventually leads Sutton-Smith (2008) to the larger conclusion that play itself is paradoxical. *The Ambiguity of Play* raises a further question that is only partially answered by his rhetorics: what exactly are the sources of obscurity within play that leave room for such divergent interpretations? Alongside the ambiguity between discourses of play, there is also an obscurity that gives rise to that ambiguity. Obscurity here is a positive phenomenon, one that offers insight into the paradoxes and aporias that shape experiences of play.

Sutton-Smith takes up obscurity in the introduction to *The Ambiguity of Play* as his motive for the whole enquiry. He suggests three reasons for play's obscurity, each based in a source of 'diversity' within it. First, he argues that play names a huge number of things and its obscurity results from that diversity of practices. Second, he describes the diversity of players who understand play differently depending on their age, gender, levels of intensity, genre expectations, capacity for self-reflection and much else. To these first two obscurities he adds a third derived from the diverse theories that academics use to analyse play. In Sutton-Smith's three introductory problems, play's obscurity goes beyond the issue of rhetoric. Indeed, in the decade of writing preceding *The Ambiguity of Play*, Sutton-Smith is preoccupied with these epistemological problems, and they structure his historical and ideological critique of play rhetoric.

This essay interrogates play's obscurity by returning to the methodological questions that motivate Sutton-Smith. To do so, I draw on my background in literary criticism and bring to bear a hermeneutic practice that illuminates the interconnections between obscurity and ambiguity. In this interpretive tradition, the act of reading is neither transparent nor neutral, but a site for close attention to the ways language constructs knowledge. Hermeneutics generates new readings of texts by focussing on aspects that can go ignored if one is primarily looking for content or results. This might include the rhetorical framing of the introduction and conclusion; the use of genre conventions from different disciplines; the ambiguity of certain grammatical constructions; the cultural associations and connotations of a phrase; changes and continuities in an author's writing style; intertextual references within a body of work; and much else. Equally, the standards of evaluation and truth in hermeneutics differ from the experimental or qualitative sciences. In a humanistic approach, a text has no single, correct meaning but neither is interpretation left up to the individual. Each text is the subject of an infinite conversation in which people share insights and arguments across multiple perspectives. There are many criteria for judging a good interpretation: how well it unifies contradictory aspects of a text; how much of a text's minutia it brings under a single umbrella; how it accounts for the genesis and evolution of a text's composition; how original and provocative the reading is; or how it situates authorial decisions within larger social and political structures. Taking an interpretive approach to *The Ambiguity of Play* does not mean evaluating Sutton-Smith's theory for its accuracy about play but producing new understandings of his argument.

The reading I propose puts Sutton-Smith's discovery of obscurity front and centre, and treats the resulting aporias as positive, deep, and hard-won insights rather than mere limitations on knowledge. Moreover, this is an iconoclastic reading insofar as I take obscurity to be the central insight of *The Ambiguity of Play*. I treat the seven rhetorics that make up the book's main chapters as, at best, a way of working-through obscurity, and at worst as a distraction from its import. My reading thus pushes against Sutton-Smith's own understanding of his writing at the time of its publication—I note later how he revises that view. Fidelity to authorial intention is only one possible metric for an accurate interpretation, one that is impossible to validate, and that often masks other ideological values (Foucault, 1979). I am more committed to the affect of surprise when a previously dull passage reveals hidden connections, to interpretations that have far-reaching consequences for play, and to correcting for an overly typological reading of Sutton-Smith's rhetorics.

To say a little more on that last point, this essay belongs to a wider project of re-evaluating canonical texts of game studies and disrupting an overly typological impulse. By a typological impulse, I mean a focus on categorizing play-theories into one of Sutton-Smith's seven broad buckets. That style of reading exhausts itself by identifying the correct play rhetoric, reduces the play-theory under consideration to something ideological, and simultaneously reduces play's ambiguity to a ready-made selection. Elsewhere I have argued against a similar approach to defining play formally in Johan Huizinga's *Homo Ludens* that can only ask whether a given situation is or is-not play (McDonald 2019). I have also deconstructed Roger Caillois's typology of games in *Man, Play and Games* to show how they emerge from his idiosyncratic background in anthropology and Surrealism (McDonald 2020). A typological reading hides the smaller-scale acts of historical interpretation that underpin all three of these texts as they discover subtle signs of playfulness. To bring out the hermeneutic strategies Brian Sutton-Smith uses to develop play rhetorics—discover their historical roots, draw their boundaries, recognize their tell-tale signs—requires an equally sensitive interpretive method.

By treating play as deeply obscure, hard to grasp, and metamorphic, the interpretive strategies that Brian Sutton-Smith develops to stabilize play come into view. However, he has no monopoly on the trouble of defining play, a task that is regularly characterized as impossible. One can call to mind Ludwig Wittgenstein's *Philosophical Investigations* (1953) where games are a key example of a word whose meaning is always contextual and plural; or Helen Schwartzman's (1978) account of all the researchers exasperated at play's flux; or Jesper Juul's (2005) attempt to reconcile seven disparate definitions of games in the early days of video game studies. Judging by the continued attempts to define and redefine play, the issue has not yet been settled (Trammell, 2020).

Sutton-Smith's work, however, offers unique benefits for asking about play's obscurity. While other scholars have thought in complex ways about the difficulties in defining play, they are typically interested in doing so either to subsequently establish a better definition or to invite consideration of a wider range of phenomena that should be included in that definition. *The Ambiguity of Play* involves, instead, sceptical questioning with no assurance that anything tangible will remain at the end. Moreover, Sutton-Smith's scepticism is born from his realization that a lifetime of work has been directed by the ideological pressures of enlightenment humanism, Romanticism, and the Protestant work ethic (Sutton-Smith, 1984b, 1993b). By the 1990s, Sutton-Smith lost his taste for ready-to-hand answers, and instead lets the methodological problems of defining play grow and complicate. It makes his work an excellent place to think about the nature of play's obscurity. In my reading, Sutton-Smith shows the value of directly engaging the paradoxes of play.

In what follows I look at the three sources of obscurity that Sutton-Smith names in the introduction to *The Ambiguity of Play* and trace their roots in his work. Each one involves difficult epistemological puzzles that are not obvious at first glance and, to some extent, remain unsolved by the book's end. Each one, begins within the same simple image of the early 20th century psychologist, Jean Piaget observing his children as they loll their head, blow spit bubbles, or breath through smushed-up noses. Piaget's description of play in *Play, Dreams, and Imitation in Childhood* (1962) was a touchstone for Sutton-Smith, who engaged Piaget in public dialogue and criticism about it during his early career. Subsequently, Sutton-Smith considers and reconsiders Piaget's observations, wondering how he makes distinctions that count some acts as play and not others. Piaget's acts of interpretation bring play into the realm of scientific inquiry, but the conditions of that judgment are obscure.

By looking closely at Brian Sutton-Smith's attempts to define and recognize play, and by following his injection of scepticism, we will see how new interpretive categories arise from the confrontation with obscurity. Reading against a simple typology of play rhetorics, I argue that Sutton-Smith pioneers a historically situated reading practice, and that his approach must be undertaken anew when shifting among play activities, players, and play disciplines.

OBSCURITY IN THE DIVERSITY OF PRACTICES

The first source of obscurity comes from the great diversity of things we call play. The list of activities Sutton-Smith generates is too long to include here, and it is not obvious what he wants the reader to understand from that list.

It includes phenomena such as 'daydreams . . . imagination . . . hobbies . . . listening to records . . . playing tricks . . . playing second fiddle . . . joking . . . travel . . . losing weight . . . playing music . . . being a play actor . . . birthdays . . . gambling . . . arm wrestling . . . [and] sky jumping' (Sutton-Smith, 1997, pp. 4–5). Sutton-Smith presents these items as things that are 'often said to be play' and does not try to discriminate further between what is really play and what is only a loose metaphor or an etymological quirk. Now, this is certainly an eclectic assortment of items, but it is questionable whether that diversity presents a real challenge to understanding play.

Only at the conclusion, when Sutton-Smith argues for new criteria that should govern the future of play theory, do we gain a sense of how his initial list undermines existing definitions. Three of his criteria bear directly on the kinds of activities that we choose to exemplify play. Play should 'include passive or vicarious forms' in contrast to definitions of play that emphasize its active nature; play should 'not be defined only in terms of the restricted modern Western values that say it is nonproductive, rational, voluntary, and fun' but should account for anthropological evidence that play can be useful, absurd, forced, and painful; and a definition should account for play that is 'as momentary as a piece of wit' and that can be 'as diffuse as a daydream' in contrast to play definitions that assert fixed boundaries in time and space (Sutton-Smith, 1997, pp. 218–19). In light of these principles, we can see Sutton-Smith's introductory list of activities as a provocation to imagine play more broadly than the formal definitions of writers like Johan Huizinga or Roger Caillois. Still, the source of obscurity eludes us. Granted that prior authors have not given play a wide enough scope to account for ordinary language, that is only an accidental limitation. A real obscurity requires that the challenge of defining play be an active force, complicating things for the play theorist whether or not they happen to agree with Huizinga.

Sutton-Smith's emphasis on passive, internal, and imaginative experience, however, points us to deeper questions about the impossibility of defining play that stem from his earlier work. In the 1980s, he was not nearly so accepting of diverse activities as play. In fact, he draws firm and clear distinctions between play and three other behaviours. First, he repeatedly contrasts play to the tentative explorations that precede it, where an infant tests out an object to discover its uses and surprises (Sutton-Smith, 1974). Second, he contrasts play to the process of gaining skills through repeated practice at moving a limb or working out all the possible ways objects might fit together (Sutton-Smith, 1986). Finally, he contrasts play with personal reverie of undirected and associative thought that does not need to accommodate itself to anything in the outside world (Sutton-Smith, 1968). Exploration, mastery, and daydreaming are three ways of dividing play from what is not-play and they all have their roots in Sutton-Smith's reading of Piaget.

In *Play, Dreams and Imitation in Childhood* (1962), Piaget argues that infantile adaptation to the world consists of two general dynamics: accommodation and assimilation. Accommodation is a process by which the infant changes to fit the contours of a situation, adding detail to existing mental schema, or abandoning assumptions that no longer make sense in the face of new evidence. Assimilation, by contrast, imposes the infant's existing viewpoint on the world, forcing round pegs into square holes, and ignoring details that do not align with preconceptions. For Piaget, pure accommodation results in imitation and an impulse to repeat the actions of other people. While Piaget does not distinguish between exploration and mastery, both elements are visible in such imitation. For instance, when an infant sees a parental gesture, accidentally moves its hand to its mouth in mimicry, and attempts to make that gesture happen a second time, that sequence is an example of both bodily exploration and newfound control. Piaget distinguishes play as the opposite of imitation, and he understands it as a pure process of assimilation that gives free reign to the infant's imagination. In play the child can treat a block as if it were something radically different—a parent, a telephone, a car—by disregarding its actual qualities and uses.

While Sutton-Smith believes that Piaget underestimates the productive role of play in learning and emotional development, he nonetheless accepts the basic division between initial, exploratory skill acquisition and its subsequent elaboration in play (Beresin et al., 2018; Sutton-Smith, 1966, 1974). It persists as binary in his thinking up until *The Ambiguity of Play*. To that first distinction between play and exploration/mastery, Sutton-Smith adds a second division between play and daydreaming that derives from a later reconsideration of *Play, Dreams, and Imitation in Childhood*. After reviewing his disagreements with Piaget, Sutton-Smith acknowledges that they may simply be talking about separate phenomena. He suggests that Piaget's pure assimilation is actually closer to reverie, with its dreamlike qualities, than to play. While this revision is explicitly about assimilation and accommodation, implicitly Sutton-Smith also contrasts play and daydreaming. For instance, he ponders whether Piaget is describing play or daydreams when he recounts, 'T . . . throwing his head back to look at familiar things from new positions . . . [and at 23 or 24 weeks] he seemed to repeat this movement with ever increasing enjoyment and ever decreasing interest in external results' (1983, p. 237). His division between play and reverie stands in stark contrast with *The Ambiguity of Play*, where daydreaming is repeatedly cited as an important aspect of play.

I read Sutton-Smith's transition from clear-cut distinctions to an open-list of play activities as a sign that he increasingly appreciates the vagueness of infantile observation and its dependence on the researcher's positionality.

Play, exploration, and reverie are not behaviours that can be easily defined through concrete actions, unlike eating for example, but only become recognizable through close attention to other actions and context. Play and exploration might be separable in adults, but in infants the boundaries are permeable. Moreover, as Sutton-Smith argues in *Toys as Culture* (1986), play is itself a skill that infants need to develop. He compares early play behaviour to infantile babble. Just as babble is language that is not really language, early play is an approximation rather than a ready-made category of behaviour. For Sutton-Smith, defining play in infantile life comes up against several obscurities: the fluid boundaries between unformed behaviours, the flux of rapid growth, and the muteness of the pre-verbal child.

While the obscurity of infant play may not account for all the variability of play's multitudinous forms, it gives us an example of how ambiguity is inherent to play rather than an accidental mistake in its theorization. It also gives us a sense of the positive contribution that obscurity can make. To assert a blanket distinction between exploration and play on theoretical grounds blinds us to the ways play might need to grow into itself. By accepting its fundamental obscurity, we can pay attention to the relational processes of observation from which each interpretation of an infant's playfulness stems.

OBSCURITY IN THE DIVERSITY OF PLAYERS

In the late 1980s, Brian Sutton-Smith attempts a second strategy for transforming play into a stable object of research. Rather than relying on definitions, one can simply expect observers to know play when they see it. For instance, Sutton-Smith (1989) describes a 'maxim in recent play psychology that researchers can reach a consensus on their perception that play is being observed, even when they cannot define what it is they are seeing' (p. 189). He notes a similar trend among observers of animal play, such as Robert Fagen, to get down to the work of observation without waiting for a specific definition (Sutton-Smith, 1997, pp. 2, 20). However, that seemingly simple act of agreement conceals its own practical, empirical, and epistemological problems. These include issues of subcultural differences, expertise, and player perspectives.

When Sutton-Smith lists the diversity of players in *The Ambiguity of Play*, it is no idle speculation but comes directly from a series of studies by his PhD students Mary Ann Magee and Kathleen Connor that examined how people categorize examples of play. While these studies started with the goal of identifying new micro-categories of play interaction, they found that certain kinds of play were difficult for observers to agree about (Sutton-Smith & Magee, 1989). Play-fighting, in particular, provoked divergent reactions, with some observers identifying it as play while others saw it as conflict. Here is the first problem with defining play based on a shared communal agreement: such agreement may not exist. Without some external criteria intervening to decide whether play-fighting is play or not, it will remain ambiguous.

The issue that Sutton-Smith and his students highlight, however, is more serious. The disagreement over play-fighting was not haphazard but systematically correlated with traits of the observers (Sutton-Smith, 2005; Sutton-Smith et al., 1988). His student found that women are more likely to classify play-fighting as conflict than men, that teachers are similarly inclined, and that people who engaged in play-fighting as children—regardless of gender or profession—are more likely to class it as play (Connor, 1991). Sutton-Smith has some explanations for these variations, citing the relation of gender norms to violence, how play-fighting disrupts classrooms, and the observer's identification with the player. For my purposes, it is the systematic nature of the different interpretations that matters because it shows that the ambiguity in playfighting is not accidental or one that could be easily resolved with further dialogue. Different communities hold fundamentally different interpretations of what play looks like and what it means.

Now, that diversity of understanding is not necessarily a problem; one could simply accept that 'play' is a word with many incompatible meanings. At the conclusion of *The Ambiguity of Play*, however, Sutton-Smith (1997) argues that a true idea of play must be a universal one. As he sees it, play is not a phenomenon that emerges from within specific cultures or sub-cultures, but a biological inheritance that we share with all mammals. It is inflected by culture, but if we can recognize the play of dogs and mice then there must be some common core of experience that unites all players. Alongside this biological argument, Sutton-Smith also presents a second thesis to support play's universality: that it is a type of communication. Sutton-Smith (1982) follows writers like Gregory Bateson (1972) and Catherine Garvey (1977) who argue that play precedes spoken language both in evolutionary terms and developmentally. If we use play to communicate, then play-fighting is not just a word within the English language that groups can define according to their own unique needs. Instead, the meaning of 'play' is always larger than its role in a community's discursive practices, because play is a condition for generating any shared understanding in the first place. Defining play according to its observers thus leads to a tension between its universal pretensions and the empirical fact of a disagreement.

If the hypothesis that we know play when we see it does not hold up in general, there might still be ways to save a more limited version of it. One could argue that only expert observers should be trusted to recognize play, with expertise presumably vested in the psychologists and biologists doing the research. To think about this possibility, Sutton-Smith (1986) turns again to look at Jean Piaget as the exemplar of a 'brilliantly insightful observer' of play (p. 142). In *Toys as Culture* (1986), he comments on Piaget's ability to recognize these moments of ambiguous infantile play but distinguishes between Piaget's questionable observations of an anonymous infant and his 'clearer' understanding of his own children at two months (p. 135). Sutton-Smith implies that it is a deep familiarity—indeed a familial relation—that allows one to be an expert, because it provides a context for judging how some tiny actions stand out as more playful than others.

Sutton-Smith makes a more theoretical version of this point in his 1983 essay on Piaget, where he suggests that these infantile observations are undermined precisely when Piaget tries to adopt a scientific attitude. Piaget takes the infant as a unit of analysis and implicitly treats play as a solitary activity. He thus excludes his wife's role in scaffolding play through "tickling, turn taking in noise making, contests with hair pulling and fingers in mouths, choral rhythmic activity with jiggling and singing together, the cumulatively exciting games of 'Peekaboo!' and 'This Little Piggy'" (Sutton-Smith, 1983, p. 244). Equally, and in line with criteria of scientific objectivity, Piaget assumes that his own presence makes no difference to the infant's play, even though his child may well be performing uniquely for him. Equally, Piaget's interpretations rely on the willingness and generosity of a father to see intelligence and joy in an infant's ambiguous acts. In Sutton-Smith's (1980b) argument, the communicative and observer-dependent aspects of play are inseparable from its definition and are crucial to play's development. Vesting the ability to define play in an expert, especially a scientist, fails because it cannot account for the interpersonal dimension of that recognition.

That relational dynamic, however, suggests a final way to save the thesis that "we know play when we see it" by focusing on players' own account of their activity. In anthropology the use of a group's self-understanding is known as an emic perspective, and Sutton-Smith briefly tries to adopt it in the study of a preschool. Asking children about their own play, however, only pushes the problem in a new direction: they refuse to draw boundaries that would be useful for studying play. As he writes:

> When we asked children to watch their own tapes and tell us when they were playing and when they were not, they did not make these same distinctions . . . Although to us the children might often seem to be engaged in nonplay negotiations, or to be alone or just onlookers, they saw themselves as playing . . . They

seem to move rather loosely about a number of quite different sorts of activities, all of which they can incorporate as being in play

(Sutton-Smith & Magee, 1989, p. 54).

Now, this is not simply an inability to say anything about play, as the children distinguished not-play activities that were imposed by adults. Rather, the labile quality comes from having an established play community at the preschool. Organizing players, negotiating a social pact, leaving a group, and later returning can all be understood as part of play in a broad sense. Sutton-Smith and Mary Ann Magee (1989) argue that play simultaneously encompasses traditional games of make-believe and the 'publicly managed performance' of a shared social space (p. 61). In other words, the process of consensus by which people come to an agreement over what is recognizably play can be absorbed into the play sphere. For the preschool children, knowing play when we see it is another kind of game.

Sutton-Smith toys with epistemological standpoints from which we might recognize play—as shared implicit knowledge, as viewed by experts, as players report it—but in each case he discovers an obscurity that stems from play itself. Play is fragmented and subject to diverse interpretations: observers cannot escape their own deep history of games, their involvement as an active and playful audience, or the idiosyncratic social rules that create play frames. At the same time, and counterbalancing that fragmentation, play is also a means for establishing contact across difference, creating an initial bond between players, and erecting a shared world. It is like language in this regard, whose exemplars are always specific and diverse, but which creates the possibility of connection. Play is obscure, then, because it always points simultaneously to the variety of existing games and to a horizon of potential new ways of playing.

The obscurity that develops from the variety of players is not accidental, but essential to the nature of play as a shared biological heritage and a communicative medium. It can only be avoided by freezing play's historical development and ignoring the specificity of each play community. But that obscurity is a resource, and there is no need to avoid it. Obscurity allows play to transform, to speak anew to each group of players, and shape itself to their needs.

OBSCURITY IN THE DIVERSITY OF DISCIPLINES

The third source of diversity, and hence ambiguity, in Sutton-Smith's account comes from the plethora of theories about play. While the remainder of *The*

Ambiguity of Play will cast that diversity as the result of 'rhetorics' that exist across Western society, the introduction begins by linking them specifically to academic disciplines. He argues that:

> Different academic disciplines also have quite different play interests. Some study the body, some study behavior, some study thinking, some study groups or individuals, some study experience, some study language—and they all use the word *play* for these quite different things (emphasis in original)
>
> (Sutton-Smith, 1997, 6).

He goes on to give examples of how these disciplinary interests shape and govern the activities that exemplify play (i.e. the first source of diversity) and the kinds of players they recognize (i.e. the second source of diversity). When Sutton-Smith frames his seven rhetorics, academic disciplines serve as the primary communities who speak for each one. The progress rhetoric belongs with the 'psychological, biological, and educational disciplines,' fate belongs to the mathematical theory of probability, power belongs to sociologists and historians, and so on (Sutton-Smith, 1997, 49).

I see Sutton-Smith's attention to disciplinarity and his disillusionment with academic norms as part of a broader re-evaluation of his own career. In 1977 he moved from the department of developmental psychology at Columbia University to the University of Pennsylvania, where he taught in the departments of education and folklore. He recounts feeling an epistemic unmooring during that relocation, particularly in his interactions with graduate students where he, 'had some difficulty in even hearing what those folklore students were saying . . . They were interested in the quality and character of play performances in the contexts in which they took place . . . not interested in abstractions about individual players [from psychology]' (Sutton-Smith, 1994, 10). These students pushed Sutton-Smith to recognize presuppositions and methodological assumptions in his own work. For instance, he organized a conference in 1977 around the theme of play and learning but discovered that the participants 'were speaking past' one another because they adhered to different play theories. A psychological camp saw play as solitary, voluntary, and involving toys; while an anthropological camp understood it as 'a form of human communication that reflects the enculturative process' (Sutton-Smith, 1980a, 6). Elsewhere Sutton-Smith draws a line between the natural sciences, which produce good experiments but struggle with their implications and the interpretive sciences, which do the converse (Sutton-Smith, 1984b). All these distinctions, and his personal investments in academia, inform the disciplinary framework of *The Ambiguity of Play*.

The bulk of Sutton-Smith's critical attention is focused on developmental psychology, and particularly the legacy of Piaget. For instance, in a

1995 essay he reflects on two metaphors that guide this field: scaffolding and structure. He argues that the idea of scaffolding 'helps to encourage . . . a mechanistic faith' in the lawlike nature of development, while the idea of structure derived from Piaget provides a teleological and predictive model that privileges 'civilized outcomes over the primitive beginnings' so that children 'ensure our future, if no longer our salvation.' (Sutton-Smith, 1995, 71 & 73). In a co-authored piece titled 'The Elusive Historical Child,' he extends these criticisms to argue that developmental psychology must be radically transformed to incorporate historical and social situations of children (Cahan et al., 1993). This means investigating children in naturalistic settings rather than laboratories, drawing on deep individual case studies of children in the manner of Piaget's account of infantile play, and turning to experiments with action research methods in schools. These insights equally apply to the psychology of play, where he begins criticizing its optimism, individualism, and evolutionary narratives (Sutton-Smith, 1992).

Sutton-Smith's seven rhetorics emerge over the course of the 1980s and 1990s in several tentative groupings. I read his categorizing impulse as an attempt to understand play's other obscurities within a larger conceptual framework. Consider how developmental psychology led to difficulty distinguishing play from other behaviours in the earliest moments of infantile life, as we saw above. This is an example where an inherent obscurity of play only becomes intelligible within a disciplinary framework. In other words, the need to define play or come to a consensus about it arises when play presents a problem to disciplinary knowledge. A clear definition in psychology helps make the instances of play countable, makes comparison possible between children, and to draw contrasts of its function across developmental stages. Conversely, a definition of play only counts as such because it answers the disciplinary needs of researchers (Meckley, 2015). If a schoolteacher needs to distinguish play from fighting, they will seek out a definition that cuts that specific knot. The situational needs of different researchers thus encounter problems and obscurities within play that would otherwise be invisible.

To take a second example, as a folklorist Sutton-Smith often wrestles another type of obscurity in play that has to do with judging the line between the playful and the serious. He writes: '[i]f I am then asked to tell you whether not being serious is play or not, I must answer that it is one of characteristics of informal play to switch in and out of everyday life in just such a labile and difficult to define manner' (Sutton-Smith, 1987, 285). This leads him to discuss anthropological examples that blur play and deadly serious action, where losers are beheaded and war operates as sport. Indeed, throughout the 1980s, as Sutton-Smith (1993a) considers more violent and non-consensual modes of play, he regularly draws on ethnographic data to disrupt the 'rhetoric' that play is uniquely free, empowering, and pleasurable in ways that are difficult for Western audiences to understand.

We could expand on this point to speculate about obscurities that different disciplines encounter within play. Animal ethology is certain that mammals and birds play, less confident about reptiles, but also speculates about whether fish and invertebrates might also have their own variations (Burghardt et al., 2015; Zylinski, 2015). Writing about art and literature identifies playful stylistic features in the text, but is less certain what it means to attribute such qualities to inanimate objects. Philosophers from Kant to Derrida have posited a kind of transcendental play as a way of describing a fundamental uncertainty in the world, but it is obscure what connection that might have to the everyday games that people engage in. Sutton-Smith is aware of all these problems, though he does not explore them in any depth.

Even this brief survey of discipline specific problems shows how they make visible new aporia of play. In this light, play theories are not partial or ideological rhetorics that could be abandoned in favour of a totalizing approach, because it is only within these traditions that real problems about play can be framed. This third obscurity brings us to the limits of *The Ambiguity of Play*. Play seems to have a relation to knowledge, to mastery, to rhetoric, and to discipline; it seems to entangle these concepts with its own being. However, it is never clear why. In my view, Sutton-Smith outlines this problem through the rhetorics of play without ever quite illuminating the real source of obscurity. Even so, this is a hard-won insight that shows us something about play: that it is self-theorizing and self-rhetorizing. Only by undertaking a vast project to think synthetically about play does this problem even come into view.

IN CONCLUSION

The ambiguity of play practices, players, and play theories tells us something about play's inherent obscurity. As Sutton-Smith writes, 'over the years it became clear to me that much of play was by itself—in its very nature, we might say—intentionally ambiguous . . . regardless of these seven general cultural frames' (2008, 118). That, however, is a belated re-reading and re-interpretation of his own work. The concluding chapter to *The Ambiguity of Play* is both more despairing and more hopeful. More despairing because the rhetorics make a unified idea of play harder to reach. He writes that '[i]f in consequence [of elucidating the seven rhetorics] there is less ambiguity about play, it would have to be because the sheer irreconcilability of these different play complexes is clearer' (Sutton-Smith, 1997, 216). More hopeful because he thinks it is at least possible to move beyond the various rhetorics towards a 'more central definition or more universal rhetoric' (1997, 217).

Sutton-Smith ends by proposing a new theory of adaptive variability based on play's evolutionary history.

This essay ends with an inversion of those emphases, and a celebration of play's obscurity. If it is in the very nature of play to obscure itself, to tease, to blur boundaries, to mask fighting as play, and to slowly emerge out of infantile stuttering, then uncovering those epistemological conundrums is a central task for play theory. The impossibility of a single definition of play need not lead to melancholy, it simply opens play to the infinite task of interpretation and re-interpretation. Rather than stabilizing play in a fixed biological, psychological, or cultural function, its obscurities render it labile and poetic. Its meaning shifts in subtle ways that cannot be predicted in advance, it transforms historically and adapts for new communities, it engulfs our theories with a laugh. A deeper understanding of its obscurities cannot pin down play into a single definition, but it can help us look for and track how it changes.

The suggestion that play is a kind of poetry to be interpreted is visible in the opening pages of *The Ambiguity of Play*. Even before offering an account of the three types of diversity, Sutton-Smith cites William Empson's text of literary criticism, *Seven Types of Ambiguity* (1955) to argue that play engages in all of them. Play contains:

1. the ambiguity of reference (is that a pretend sound, or are you choking?);
2. the ambiguity of referent (is that an object or a toy?);
3. the ambiguity of intent (do you mean that, or is it pretend?);
4. the ambiguity of sense (is this serious, or is it nonsense?);
5. the ambiguity of transition (you said you were only playing?);
6. the ambiguity of contradiction (a man playing at being a woman);
7. the ambiguity of meaning (is it play or playfighting?)

(Sutton-Smith, 1997, 2).

Sutton-Smith offers these analogies between play and literary language but never comments on them or returns to them. However, they suggest a way of understanding the book's larger project as an interpretive one. Play is dense and layered, deeply dependent on the context of its creation and its reception, always revealing new meanings to those who are willing to look closely. Holding onto the obscurity of play is the first step towards engaging its poetry.

REFERENCES

Bateson, G. (1972) *Steps to an ecology of the mind*. New York, Ballantine.

Beresin, A., Brown, F., & Patte, M. M. (2018). Brian Sutton-Smith's Views on Play. In J. L. Roopnarine & P. K. Smith (Eds.), *The Cambridge Handbook of Play: Developmental and Disciplinary Perspectives* (pp. 383–398). Cambridge University Press.

Burghardt, G. M., Dinets, V., & Murphy, J. B. (2015). Highly repetitive object play in a cichlid fish (Tropheus duboisi). *Ethology, 121*(1), 38–44.

Cahan, E., Mechling, J., Sutton-Smith, B., & White, S. H. (1993). The elusive historical child: Ways of knowing the child of history and psychology. In G. Elder, J. Modell, & R. Parke (Eds.), *Children In Time and Place–Development and Historical Insights* (pp. 192–223). Cambridge University Press.

Connor, K. (1991). *War toys, aggression and playfighting* [Doctoral dissertation, University of Pennsylvania]. Proquest Dissertations. https://www.proquest.com/dissertations-theses/war-toys-aggression-playfighting/docview/303957083/se-2

Foucault, M. (1979). What is an author? *Screen, 20*(1), 13–34.

Garvey, C. (1977). *Play.* London: Fontana.

Juul, J. (2005). *Half-Real: Video Games between Real Rules and Fictional Worlds.* MIT Press.

McDonald, P. (2019). Homo Ludens: A renewed reading. *American Journal of Play* 11(2), 247–267.

McDonald, P. (2020). The principle of division in Roger Caillois's Man, Play and Games. *Games and Culture* 15(8), 855–873.

Meckley, A. M. (2015). *A Student's Guide for Understanding Play Through the Theories of Brian Sutton-Smith: Vol. II* (J. E. Johnson, S. G. Eberle, T. S. Henricks, & D. Kuschner, Eds.; pp. 393–405). Rowman & Littlefield.

Piaget, J. (1962). *Play, Dreams, and Imitation in Childhood.* Routledge & Kegan Paul.

Schwartzman, H. (1979). *Transformations: The Anthropology of Children's Play.* Plenum Press.

Suits, B. (2014). *The Grasshopper: Games, Life and Utopia* (3rd ed.). Broadview Press.

Sutton-Smith, B. (1966). Piaget on play: A critique. *Psychological Review, 73*(1), 104–110.

Sutton-Smith, B. (1968). Games—Play—Daydreams. *Quest, 10*(1), 47–58.

Sutton-Smith, B. (1974). Play as novelty training. In J. Andrews (Ed.), *One Child Indivisible* (pp. 227–258). National Association for the Education of Young Children.

Sutton-Smith, B. (1980a). A 'Sportive' Theory of Play. In H. B. Schwartzman (Ed.), *Play and Culture* (pp. 10–18). Leisure Press.

Sutton-Smith, B. (1980b). Children's Play: Some Sources of Play Theorizing. *New Directions for Child Development, 9*, 1–16.

Sutton-Smith, B. (1982). A Performance Theory of Peer Relations. In K. Borman (Ed.), *The Social Life of Children in a Changing Society* (pp. 65–77). Lawrence Erlbaum Asscociates.

Sutton-Smith, B. (1983). Piaget, Play, and Cognition, Revisited. In W. F. Overton (Ed.), *The relationship between social and cognitive development* (pp. 229–250). Lawrence Erlebaum Asscociates.

Sutton-Smith, B. (1984a). Text and context in imaginative play and the social sciences. *New Directions for Child Development*, *25*, 53–70.

Sutton-Smith, B. (1984b). The Origins of Fiction and the Fictions of Origin. In E. Bruner & S. Plattner (Eds.), *Text, play, and story: The construction and reconstruction of self and society* (pp. 117–132). Waveland Press.

Sutton-Smith, B. (1986). *Toys as Culture*. Gardner Press.

Sutton-Smith, B. (1987). School Play: A Commentary. In J. H. Block & N. R. King (Eds.), *School Play: A Source Book* (pp. 277–290). Teachers College Press.

Sutton-Smith, B. (1989). Introduction to Play as Performance, Rhetoric, and Metaphor. *Play & Culture*, *2*(3), 189–192.

Sutton-Smith, B. (1992). Notes Towards a Critique of Twentieth-Century Psychological Play Theory. *Homo Ludens: Der Spielende Mensch*, *2*, 95–107.

Sutton-Smith, B. (1993a). Suggested Rhetorics in Adult Play Theories. *Play Theory & Research*, *1*(2), 102–116.

Sutton-Smith, B. (1993b). Dilemmas in Adult Play with Children. In K. MacDonald (Ed.), *Parent-Child Play: Descriptions and Implications* (pp. 15–40). State University of New York Press.

Sutton-Smith, B. (1994). Paradigms of Intervention. In J. Hellendoorn, R. van der Kooij, Amsterdam Play Symposium, & B. Sutton-Smith (Eds.), *Play and intervention* (pp. 3–22). State University of New York Press.

Sutton-Smith, B. (1995). Radicalizing childhood: The multivocal mind. In H. McEwan & K. Egan (Eds.), *Narrative in teaching, learning, and research* (pp. 69–90). Teacher's College Press.

Sutton-Smith, B. (1997). *The Ambiguity of Play*. Harvard University Press.

Sutton-Smith, B. (2008). Play Theory: A Personal Journey and New Thoughts. *American Journal of Play*, *1*(1), 80–123.

Sutton-Smith, B. (2005). Courage in the Playground: A Tribute to Dorothy Howard. In K. Darian-Smith & J. Factor (Eds.), *Child's Play: Dorothy Howard and the Folklore of Australian Children* (pp. 187–203). Museum Victoria.

Sutton-Smith, B., Gerstmyer, J., & Meckley, A. (1988). Playfighting as Folkplay amongst Preschool Children. *Western Folklore*, *47*, 161–176.

Sutton-Smith, B., & Kelly-Byrne, D. (1984). The Idealization of Play. In P. K. Smith (Ed.), *Play in animals and humans* (pp. 305–321). Blackwell.

Sutton-Smith, B., & Magee, M. A. (1989). Reversible Childhood. *Play & Culture*, *2*(1), 52–63.

Trammell, A. (2020). Torture, play, and the black experience. *G|A|M|E Games as Art, Media, Entertainment*, *1*(9), 33–49.

William, E. (1947). *Seven Types of Ambiguity*. New Directions.

Wittgenstein, L. (2009). *Philosophical Investigations* (4th ed.). John Wiley & Sons.

Zylinski, S. (2015). Fun and play in invertebrates. *Current Biology*, *25*(1), R10–R12.

Chapter 4

Key Ideas of Brian Sutton-Smith

Anna Beresin

In *Keywords: A Vocabulary of Culture and Society* Raymond Williams presented over 100 significant words in use in the social sciences and humanities. In honor of Brian's own significant contribution to the way we think about play, I offer a Sutton-Smynthesis of Brian's own key ideas, a brief list of his keywords or phrases that are, in my opinion, his most important. Some of his ideas became book titles, but others emerged through the folklore within academic circles, savored and repeated in our own oral tradition. See how each reflects not only a phase of his thinking, but reflects his command of yet another academic literature. Keys unlock doors. Brian opened minds with these keys.

The key ideas here reflect his unique observations of the world of play, although Brian published widely in the general topics of developmental psychology, education, anthropology, and children's literature (Sutton-Smith, 1949; Sutton-Smith and Rosenberg, 1970; Sutton-Smith, 1979; Sutton-Smith, 1976). Unlike Raymond Williams' list, these key phrases are not keys because they are highly utilized. They are rare and not utilized enough. But in their uniqueness, they have great utility, a Swiss army knife when the door in front of you will not open.

For Raymond Williams, his list of keywords was not a dictionary, but a "record of an inquiry into a vocabulary: a shared body of words and meanings in our most general discussions" (1976, 15). Like Williams' list, this initial one is interdisciplinary, but unlike his collection, Sutton-Smith's terms have not been around long enough for their meanings to change, to offer what linguists call a semantic shift. I encountered Brian's work by stumbling over his book *Toys as Culture* in the Harvard Coop Bookstore in 1986 and decided on the spot that I would travel to Philadelphia to meet him. I became his graduate student and the phrases below are my own favorite keys, the tools I take with me wherever I go. They are not in alphabetical order, but the list has a conceptual logic and mnemonic that will be revealed at the end of this article.

DIALUDICS

Dialudic was Brian's term for the conflation of ludic, the Latin word for "play" and dialectic. In his 2008 article reprinted posthumously in 2017 he wrote, "Play as a dualistic concept (which I designate here a 'dialudic' concept) is what I plan to examine as my guiding and central metaphor" (2017, 68). "I now prefer to use my invented word dialudic for game's antithetical complexities" (2017, 42).

Previously in 1997, he shared his thinking:

> So now we have, in effect, two dialectical relationships: the one between the mundane and virtual worlds that leads to the play transformations (which I will call the referential dialectic) and the one within the play form itself, between play and the playfulness it engenders (called the ludic dialectic) (1997, 197).

Greater than his work on ambiguity, dialudics captures the tension in the process of negotiating play, reflecting the layers within layers nestled in adult power over children's time. Dialudics work socially, culturally, and emotionally.

> In general, each of the play forms I deal with can be related to a dialudic motivating emotion (such as, in this case, shock) and an antithetical performance characteristic (like resilience), this latter working to counter the damage done by the former as a result of a game (2017, 128).

Dialudics implies that play is always in process, always in tension, always in some way ambiguously social. Prior to these last books, he explored dialectical tensions and paradox in the games of order and disorder (1972), the dialectics of sports, games, and power (1977), children's cultural ritual/ innovation (1972), Freudian frivolousness/seriousness, (1981) and the toy miniaturization of large ideas (1986). Brian moved through layers to understand layers, using the idea of dialudics at play to model a rhetorical approach to scholarship itself. The *Rhetorics of Play* was the original title of *The Ambiguity of Play.* I think the former would be the more accurate one. For an excellent cheat, see his chart of play rhetorics in the conclusion of that book (1997, 215).

"AS"

Many of his articles and books utilized the word "as:" *Play as Emotional Survival, Toys as Culture, The School Playground as Festival.* He was more interested in how play served as a tool rather than define what it actually is. The word "is" somehow reduces play, and Brian was more interested in play's expansion, both conceptually and in terms of child advocacy (Hellendoorn, van der Kooij, and Sutton-Smith, 1994).

With all due respect, for Erik Erikson, play is mastery (Erikson, 1977). For Jean Piaget, play is the primacy of assimilation over accommodation (Piaget, 1951). For Brian, play has been said to be ambiguity, but I counter that he suggested that play moved in ambiguity, that ambiguity was more of Brian's own way of working with the slippery literature on play than an essential quality. He would constantly remind his students that we still do not know what play is, although he used the term "is" in metaphor. "Play is, as it were, a halfway house between the night and the day, the brain and the world" (1997, 61). Play exists in between, intentionally mysterious. He wrote, "In short we don't know why children play, even if they can't help doing it" (1997, 49).

Play plays, like all theater, as/if. He turned the as/if lens to the research literature on play, questioning the veracity of universal statements made about play's essential nature. Rooted in the word "as," Brian played with a model of thinking about the social sciences as part of the humanities, a collection of artifacts of thought, rather than facts per se. Facts were hard to find, given the abundance of play rhetoric.

TRIVIALITY BARRIER

First published in *Western Folklore* in January 1970, Brian coined the oft cited phrase "triviality barrier" to lament the under appreciation of the importance of play for those who take care of children, educate them, and even study them.

"Treating all of this play as frivolousness, as something to be put aside, illustrates and adds momentum to the idea that adults should organize the kind of play through which children are believed to develop properly" (1997, 205). He called this a hegemony of play, the privileging of some play forms over another, a parallel process to the overall scorning of play itself in Western academic culture. "In scholarship the denigration of play in intellectual terms is shown by the absence of the key term *play* from the index of almost every book about the behavior of human beings" (1997, 208).

To document the triviality barrier, he advised us to see how many teacher-training programs or psychology or anthropology curricula include courses on play. Study how much time is offered to children at school for breaktime or recess. Observe how many hours are expected for work/school time as compared to leisure. Pay attention to how cultures around the globe handle time, space, and the value of play across the lifespan. As this tribute is being written, the triviality barrier still looms large in children's education and our own higher education.

OPTIMISTIC LUDICISM

He wrote that "players need to be unrealistically optimistic (1997, 64) and that games can be considered to be "an exercise in optimism" (1997, 70). Play, particularly gambling is "a kind of existential optimism" (1997, 72).

Many of our play scholars have quoted a version of a phrase attributed to him, namely "The opposite of play is depression." The actual quote is even more powerful:

> What is adaptive about play, therefore, may be not only the skills that are a part of it but also the willful belief in acting out one's own capacity for the future. The opposite of play, in these terms, is not a present reality or work, it is vacillation, or worse, it is depression (1997, 198).

Implied here is that in order to practice optimism we need to sustain play so it sustains us.

TOYS AS CULTURE

Brian turned his anthropological lens on our own consumerist culture. He stood between the psychological literature on toys as transitional objects (Winnicott, 1971), as reflecting the body psychologically (Erikson, 1977), and toys as a form of socialization (Barthes, 1957). He was reaching for a way to link classics in the study of material culture in anthropology and look at Western culture with a visitor's eye.

Perhaps it helped that he came from New Zealand and was able to see culture where others saw the psychologically normative or universal. He was aware of the cultural uniqueness of the Māori early in his career and chronicled both indigenous and colonially-imported games. All games and toys were to be studied from an anthropological lens, and all could be examined within the larger paradoxes of miniaturization and gifting.

For this writer, the greatest significance of this book is to remind the field of psychology that there is no generic human. All objects and rules are cultural. We can even think of dreams as culture.

FOLKLORE/ FOLKSTORIES/ FOLKGAMES
OF CHILDREN

Although Brian was one of a handful of key writers in children's folklore, he was keen to distinguish those books that addressed folklore for children, meaning fairy tales and the like, and folklore of children. (Opie and Opie, 1951; 1959; 1969; 1980; 1985; 1997). Brian's main interest was in the children's folklore scholarship that focused on children's peer culture, treating their songs, movements, rituals, jokes, art and stories as seriously as one who studied adult folk cultures ethnographically. His book the *Folkstories of Children* (1972) served as a bridge between his two fields, children's folklore and developmental psychology, as he attempted to show the increasing sophistication in stories about falling down and dying and rise of fart jokes.

Folkstories of Children documented children's spontaneous storytelling, as masterful in its immaturity as any adult spinning Cinderella tales around a campfire. Children's folk storytelling had not been seriously examined as a cultural/developmental artifact, and his work further legitimized the children's cultures as serious, artful, and yet hilarious. He was particularly unusual in the delight he shared in his studies of children's lore. Much of developmental psychology had treated such material anesthetically, clinically, humorlessly in the name of science.

Folkgames of Children (1972) was a collection of his work in both New Zealand and in the U.S. divided into sections labeled "historical approaches," "anthropological approaches," "psychological approaches," and "unified approaches." The latter attempted to use tools from all of these disciplines in the study of such things as marbles and kissing games. Other edited books of his include *Children's Games Anthology: Studies in Folklore and Anthropology* (1976) and *Children's Folklore: A Sourcebook* (1995). These works paralleled his 1976 edited book on adult games, *The Games of the Americas: A Book of Readings, Part 1: Central and South America, and Part II: North America.* He insisted that any theories of play must take into account adult play as well as children's own, and that the folk cultures of children were to be taken as seriously as any adult cultures.

Children's folklore and ethnographic studies of play were likely the catalyst for his thinking of generalized play research as mostly rhetoric. How many studies of children's play, particularly when they are related to violent or unsavory themes, reflect actual scientific truths rather than rhetoric? The answers lie in careful, critical study. Even in our field of play research, too often phrases are repeated without pausing to critique. Is play really the "child's work" (Paley, 2004)? Is play always optional or freely chosen? Does play need to be purposeful in order to be valuable (Sutton-Smith, 1997)? What do the children themselves as experts in their own time and space have to say about their play? What do they value?

ADAPTIVE VARIABILITY

In looking for what is common to child and adult forms of play, to animal and human forms, to dreams, daydreams, play, games, sports and festivals, it is not hard to reach the conclusion that what they have in common, even cross culturally, is their amazing diversity and variability. The possibility then arises, that is it is this variability that is central to the function of play throughout all species. Considering that variation is also a key concept within biological thought, this seems like the most profitable point to begin the inquiry (1997, 221).

"So in conclusion, I have presented here the view that variability is the key to play, and that structurally play is characterized by quirkiness, redundancy, and flexibility" (1997, 229). He writes, "Finally, I define play as facsimilization of the struggle for survival as this is broadly rendered by Darwin . . . the potentiation of adaptive variability (1997, 231).

This adaptive variability functions for children as well as adults, "What was once hidden as daydreams now takes on the mask of the computer screen for anticipations and rehearsals . . . There can be no doubt that virtual worlds are a new play form allowing adults to play almost as amorphously as children." (1997, 178)

He was ahead of his time.

EMOTIONAL SURVIVAL

Right before his death, Brian was consumed with the idea of play as emotional survival, linking neuroscience and animal study to the study of human play. According to Darwin (1872) the primary emotions are sadness, fear, anger, joy, surprise and disgust. Brian noted that different forms of play were associated with different play forms: the "fear of physical risks" and "fear in ludic unpredictability," the "anger in contest," particularly in computer games, the "disgust of deviant play," the sadness (loneliness) countered by festivals, the "peak experiences" of play itself. (2017, 5). He intuited that our animal brains were wired to play, although he noted that animal play scholars suggest that play is "basically not to be a functional kind of behavior." (2017, 65). Here lies another paradox.

We need to play- emotionally, socially, culturally—even though play does not necessarily satisfy or prepare us for the future. We play to survive, but only indirectly. This unfinished concept of his invites us to wrestle with the key question of our need for play: What is its utility? Why do we do it? In one of our informal discussions about art therapy and play therapy he noted that the problem with therapy is that different people find different kinds of things therapeutic. Perhaps play itself in its wide net of options emotionally, physically, spiritually presents nature's own safety net for our collective survival. Future research may demonstrate neurologically how we are wired for play. But it seems ironic that we might need to prove scientifically that aesthetic, emotional experiences are good for us.

This Sutton-Smynthesis is admittedly brief, yet dense. To honor his playful spirit, I present a mnemonic device to remember his key ideas:

DIALUDICS AS TOT FAVES

Yes, this is clunky, but no more so than "My Very Excellent Mom Just Served Us Noodles," a mnemonic for memorizing the order of the planets. Or, for you readers of the treble clef, "Every Good Bird Does Fly" or my personal favorite, "Eating Green Bananas Disgusts Friends."

Dialudics
As
Triviality Barrier
Optimistic Ludicisim
Toys as Culture
Folk
Adaptive
Variability
Emotional
Survival

At the last conference that he attended at the Strong Museum of Play, we walked together through the museum exhibits as he beamed at the little ones. Tot faves.

REFERENCES

Avedon, Elliott M. and Brian Sutton-Smith. 1971. *The study of games*. Hoboken: John Wiley.

Barthes, Roland. 1957/1972. *Mythologies*. New York: Hill and Wang.

Darwin, Charles. 1872. *Expression of emotion in man and animals*. John Murray.

Erikson, Erik. 1977. *Toys and reasons*. New York: Norton.

Hellendoorn, Joop, van der Kooj, Rimmert, and Brian Sutton-Smith. 1994. *Play and intervention*. Amsterdam Play Symposium.

Herron, R. E. and Brian Sutton-Smith. 1971. *Child's play*. Hoboken: Wiley and Halstead.

Opie, Iona and Peter Opie. 1951. *The Oxford dictionary of nursery rhymes*. New York: Oxford University Press.

Opie, Iona and Peter Opie. 1959. *The lore and language of schoolchildren*. New York: Oxford University Press.

Opie, Iona and Peter Opie. 1969. *Children's games in street and playground*. New York: Oxford University Press.

Opie, Iona and Peter Opie. 1980. *The classic fairy tales*. New York: Oxford University Press.

Opie, Iona and Peter Opie.1985. *The singing game*. New York: Oxford University Press.

Opie, Iona and Peter Opie. 1997. *Children's games with things*. New York: Oxford University Press.

Paley, Vivian Gussen. 2004. *A child's work: The importance of fantasy play*. Chicago: University of Chicago Press.

Piaget, Jean. 1951. *Play, dreams and imitation in childhood*. New York: Norton.

Sutton-Smith, Brian. 1949/1961. *Smitty does a bunk*. Wellington, NZ: Price Wilburn and Co.

Sutton-Smith, Brian.1970. "The psychology of childlore: The triviality barrier." *Western Folklore*. Jan. Vol 29. 1. Pp 1–8.

Sutton-Smith, Brian.1972. "Games of order and disorder." Paper presented to the symposium on Forms of Symbolic Inversion at the American Anthropological Association, Toronto.

Sutton-Smith, Brian.1972. *Folkgames of children*. Austin: University of Texas Press.

Sutton-Smith, Brian.1976. *Games of the Americas: A book of readings*. New York: Arno Press.

Sutton-Smith, Brian. 1977. "Dialectics of play." In *Physical activity and human well-being*, edited by Fernand Landry and William Andrew Robert Orban. Miami, FL: Symposia Specialists.

Sutton-Smith, Brian. 1979. *Play and learning*. New York. Gardner Press.

Sutton-Smith, Brian. 1981. *The folkstories of children*. Philadelphia: University of Pennsylvania Press.

Sutton-Smith, Brian. 1986. *Toys as culture*. New York: Gardner Press.

Sutton-Smith, Brian. 1990. The school playground as festival. *Children's Environments Quarterly* 7 (2) 3–7.

Sutton-Smith, Brian. 1997. *The ambiguity of play*. Cambridge, MA: Harvard University Press.

Sutton-Smith, Brian. 2017. *Play for life: Play theory and play as emotional survival*. Rochester: The Strong.

Sutton-Smith, Brian, and B. G. Rosenberg 1970. *The sibling*. New York: Norton.

Sutton-Smith, Brian, Meckling, Jay, Johnson, Thomas W., and Felicia McMahon. 1995. *Children's folklore: A sourcebook*. New York: Garland.

Williams, Raymond. 1976/1983. *Keywords: A vocabulary of culture and society*. Oxford University Press

Winnicott, D.W. 1971. *Playing and reality*. New York: Basic Books.

Chapter 5

The Remembrances of a Folklorist

June Factor

Long before the internet and email, the leading English-language researchers of children's folklore kept up a steady stream of correspondence and occasional meetings. The 'mother' of the group was the innovative American scholar, Dorothy Howard. The most prolific and ultimately influential were Iona and Peter Opie in Britain. The Australian historian Ian Turner was perhaps the most radical, publishing the first uncensored collection of children's play rhymes. And then there was Brian Sutton-Smith from New Zealand and later the USA, who challenged us to revisit our thinking about the significance of play throughout the life-span.

Brian was a gifted scholar, a charismatic teacher, and a joyous colleague. Always a happy iconoclast, items from his lengthy publishing oeuvre are now de rigueur on every folklore and playlore student's and academic's reference list. His range is impressive, his refusal to succumb to an instrumentalist explanation for the ubiquity of play even more so. His insistence on nuance, on play's ambiguity and its capacity to injure as well as enhance, mark his writing as both challenging and likely to endure. Vale Brian—we honour your rich and productive life.

Chapter 6

Play Manifesto

Ana Marjanovic-Shane

CONTENT, INTENT, AND MOMENTUM

Play Manifesto is a short plea in the name of play summarizing tensions existing between conventional education and the organization of children's lives in contemporary society, on the one hand, and the value and significance of play, playfulness, and creativity needed for a good, meaningful, and healthy human life, on the other. I describe and analyze problems and challenges standing in the way of play, playfulness, and creativity in contemporary conventional schooling, and I develop a case in defense of play. I apologize, it contains serious play scholarship, but it is intended to provoke ideas on seriously changing ecologies of children's lives and education to welcome and promote play in a meaningful way. What do you think?

THE PROBLEM

Play, playfulness, and creativity may be of central importance in human life and development, both as individuals and in the development of societies and cultures, according to contemporary social scientists (Bruner & Sherwood, 1976; Graeber & Wengrow, 2021; Huizinga, 2009; Marjanović, 1977; Piaget, 1951; Sutton-Smith, 1997; Sutton-Smith et al., 2017; Vygotsky, 1976, and many others). In my view, too, they have intrinsic value for humans. However, modern industrial society has posed serious challenges to play, playfulness, and creativity. This problem is especially severe in the lives of children, although it exists for all. Because of its severity and specificity, in this manifesto, I particularly address the problems and obstacles related to play in the lives of young children.

47

Modern industrial societies around the world place a strong stress on conventional education in which play, playfulness, and creativity have been systematically suppressed and devaluated. Public education on all levels, including the earliest childhood[1], has increasingly focused on the effectiveness of teaching cognitive skills, the transmission of ready-made knowledge, pattern recognition, memorization, and training. Childhood is considered the most important time in life that should be organized around activities that enhance the child's "preparation for life" rather than left to the unpredictability and serendipity of living in the moment (*Carpe Diem*). Moreover, since "preparation for life" is the sole *raison d'être* of the usually mandated public education, this organized preparation for life is considered more valuable than "merely living" – e.g., "extremely important," "having importance of the national interest," (cf., Elmore & Fuhrman, 1990). Thus, just being, just "living," just having "free time," especially in childhood, is often seen as a waste of time. In the serious educational business of "preparation for life" – a life that will come in some distant future—there is not much place for play, playfulness, and creativity, these "frivolous," unproductive, unpredictable, and untamable activities (cf. Sutton-Smith, 1997). Nor is there a place for other kinds of leisure that are, outside of education, known to be necessary for the good life and personal enrichment, such as spending time with family and friends, engaging in the activities of personal interests and desires, having time for serendipitous encounters, dialogues, and reflections, entertainment, or just doing nothing.

According to some anthropological, sociological, and psychological studies, (Bronfenbrenner, 1981; Bruner, 1968, 1976; Bruner et al., 1976; Patte, 2009; Riesman et al., 1961; Sutton-Smith, 1972, 1973, 1976b), suppression and devaluation of play, playfulness, and personal interests and desires in early childhood seem to be just a symptom of the much more profound and larger issues caused by the fundamental changes in the current conditions for raising children in many parts of the world (Gray, 2010, 2013; Holloway & Pimlott-Wilson, 2014; Marjanović, 1987c).

CHALLENGES FOR PLAY IN THE MODERN WORLD

The contemporary social conditions in the modern Western industrial societies (and broader) in which children grow up pose serious challenges to play, playfulness, creativity, and all other forms of life that are not strictly "productive," "efficient," and understood as beneficial for children's development and their preparation for future life.

I believe the following list of societal conditions may be the most severe threats to play playfulness and creativity in childhood. If we believe that play is in some deep way central to the life of humanity in general, then these conditions and practices may also threaten some fundamental aspects of human lives in general. They may threaten the healthy, integrated, and meaningful lives in which all people, including children and youth, should be able to practice self-actualization and self-determination. However, the most challenging conditions and practices in childhood are the following:

- Segregation of children and adolescents from the rest of society into separate social groups (perhaps social classes) that spend most of their lives in special child care and educational institutions. This segregation leads to the decontextualization of childhood and adolescence from the actual socio-historical conditions and events of their lives. Once segregated and institutionalized, children's experiences of the society, its practices, the others and their lives become impoverished. Children lose opportunities to directly experience and perceive the full richness of the adults' lives, their ways of being, behaving, and relating to life, to each other, and to self. Instead, children in general, and young children in particular, spend a large proportion of their time in rather purified environments of the institutions of public education and care (Marjanović, 1987b). Lacking a substantial portion of the variety of first-hand life experiences in the life of society and its variety of communities is often a problem for overall child development. Specifically, it creates challenges for play, playfulness, and creativity. It has been known that rich play, playfulness, and creativity depend on the richness of the experience of everyday life and participation in diverse aspects of the public sphere (Calhoun, 1992; Gripsrud & Eide, 2010; Marjanović, 1987b; Sutton-Smith et al., 2017; Vygotsky, 1976, 1987, 1998). Additionally, within the institutions for early childhood education and care, children almost completely lose the freedom to play without the supervision of adults, who now keep them constantly under a spotlight (Matusov et al., 2016; Rinaldi, 1998, see more below).
- Segregation of children and youth into age groups, where younger and older children and youth lose mutual interaction. This segregation into narrow age groups (usually by the year of birth) further intensifies the impoverishment of the opportunities the children have to experience and perceive the important others, their lives and relationships, life problematics, and resolutions of their life challenges. In addition, there are many indicators that children and youth create and transmit to each other a specific youth culture throughout generations. Older children and youth initiate the younger ones into games, rituals, and children's rich lore (verbal and situational) through joint free intergenerational play and leisure time (Opie & Opie, 1967, 1969; Propp et al., 1984; Sutton-Smith,

1981; Sutton-Smith et al., 2017). Connected to this is also gender seg-regation, especially in some cultures and cultural groups. Even some games are thought appropriate only for particular genders.

- Schoolification of childhood and adolescence—reducing time for free, unsupervised activities, play, and playfulness in educational institutions, even at the preschool-age level. Studies of recess in Western public school show drastically reduced times when children can engage in unsupervised play activities (Beresin, 2010; London, 2019; Patte, 2009; Pellegrini, 2008; Ramstetter & Murray, 2017). This is accompanied by the reduced places where children can play, such as playgrounds, streets, yards, parks, etc. (Holloway & Pimlott-Wilson, 2014). Reducing oppor-tunities for play in childhood may have already led, in modern indus-trial societies, to the increase in mental problems in children and youth (Gray, 2010). In extreme cases of the impoverished institutionalized lives of babies and toddlers, the lack of playful relationships and activi-ties may even lead to severe physical and mental retardation (Brown & Webb, 2008).

- The exploitation and instrumentalization of play for educational and schooling purposes (as a result of schoolification) – creating play-like activities that serve as instruments for students' engagement in school assignments, activities that, in actuality, have little to do with play and playfulness. This instrumentalization of play could be done in many different ways: exploiting real play and games; creating pseudo-play activities for practicing particular skills; using play as a bribe for doing school work and homework; etc. In most cases, children are aware that these "educational" uses of play are draining the life out of "real" play (Beresin, 2010; Brown & Patte, 2013; Patte, 2009). It seems clear that strong tensions exist between play and education: education is trying to get on the territory of play, to subdue or exploit play. However, we do not know where the legitimate boundary between them lies. Can educa-tion and play overlap and support each other? If so, in what ways, under what circumstances, and conditions? Can education and schooling be influenced by some of the central characteristics and principles of play? I discuss these issues in more detail below, in my current assumptions and visions about play.

- Patronization of children's play. Many middle-class children in indus-trialized, Western societies live under almost constant supervision and excessive adult interference in their lives and play. Adults often create various forms of guidance for playing, choosing what they deem to be appropriate games/play and controlling their rules (Beresin, 2010; Brown & Taylor, 2008; Gladwin, 2008; Holloway & Pimlott-Wilson, 2014; Lareau, 2003; Taylor, 2008). " . . . some [children are] being channeled into commercialized play spaces and supervised clubs and activities . . . [W]hat has been lost . . . [are] children's outdoor play and independent mobility . . . [as the result of] changing socio-spatial organization of children's play" (Holloway & Pimlott-Wilson, 2014, p. 614).

- Colonization, commercialization, standardization, and typification of children's play by adults are issues related to the patronization of play. In some types of practices, the adults are in complete charge of designing ecology and the environments that channel, structure, or limit children's play, while the reasons and motives for these designs are not related to playing *per se,* having other purposes in mind. For instance, the design, architecture, and furnishing of daycare centers and playgrounds, standardization and stereotyping of toys, design of video games, etc. In addition, play and games are heavily exploited by a lucrative child and youth-focused industry (McKendrick et al., 2000; Striniste & Moore, 1989).

- Devaluation (and even demonization) of play or some forms of play. Play is seen as useless, trivial, unproductive, childish, irrelevant, and insignificant in the "serious" adult business (Sutton-Smith, 1997). The transformation in the status of children in modern society leads to the overall devaluation of children, their needs, and their ways of living. " . . . play is just fooling around, [children] asking questions is pestering, curiosity is dangerous, decisiveness is disobedience, collaboration is a nuisance, feelings are impolite, and imagination is an error in thinking" (Marjanović, 1987c, p. 24). Playing can be more than devaluated; it can even be seen as a form of addiction (playing video games, both for children and adults) that must be forbidden.

Another significant issue is the issue of children growing up in diverse cultures that may not have the same vision of play as has been developed in the social science of our modern Western culture (Rogoff, 1990; Schieffelin & Ochs, 1979, 1986). Most (but not all) of the currently known studies of play, playfulness, and creativity, predominant in contemporary views of child development, have been done within the Western philosophical, scientific, ideological, cultural, and upbringing traditions. From that point of view, what we see as the critical role or roles of play, may not coincide with different cultural traditions and their philosophical, cultural, and social beliefs. As Rogoff pointed out, "Key to moving beyond one's own system of assumptions is recognizing that goals of human development—what is regarded as mature or desirable—vary considerably according to the cultural traditions and circumstances of different communities" (Rogoff, 2003). All of that means that there exist very different understandings and concepts of the "childhood" and different practices of child-rearing and education. International cooperation focused on promoting play and playfulness could thus create opportunities for better and deeper studies of early educational practices and the role that play and playfulness can have in different local and national cultures, for children and also for adults.

THE SIGNIFICANCE OF PLAY FOR
REALIZING HUMANITY

For me, it is difficult to define play. Yet, I agree with many scholars that play is at the very heart of being human and, therefore, that play is an existential human need. In fact, play probably pre-exists humanity. According to a number of studies, some kinds of playing and playfulness are older than humanity and human cultures (Bateson, 1976; Bruner, 1976). It has been documented that some forms of play exist in mammals and potentially other species (Burghardt, 2005). But it seems to me that full-blown human play may represent an evolutionary breakthrough that opened new possibilities in human evolution. Alas, the differences between human forms and meanings of play and play in animals have not been systematically studied. However, I agree with several scholars of play that human existence as humans may be deeply related to aspects of play that maybe facilitate and set up the appearance of the crucial facets of human life, including the genesis of individual subjectivities, the development of cognitive and symbolic skills, building and creation of communities, cultures, and societies (Graeber & Wengrow, 2021; Huizinga, 2009; Marjanović, 1979, 1987a; Sutton-Smith, 1997; Sutton-Smith et al., 2017; Vygotsky, 1976, and others). I agree with Huizinga, who was probably the most influential play scholar, when he said that play,

> . . . goes beyond the confines of purely physical or purely biological activity. It is a significant function—that is to say, there is some sense to it. In play, there is something 'at play' which transcends the immediate needs of life and imparts meaning to the action. All play means something" (Huizinga, 2009, p. 1).

This is why, together with Graeber and Wengrow (2021), I tend to suspect that play and playfulness may be significantly connected to imaginative breakthroughs overcoming the status quo of the existing cultures and given conditions of life. Like Turner (1982), I find it important to think of play as "liminal." Sutton-Smith, another influential scholar of play, argued that play occupies "the threshold between reality and unreality" (Sutton-Smith, 1997, p. 1). For me, it has been important to explore the boundary between the "experience of the existing reality" and the "unreality," i.e., the boundary between the realm of "the real" and the realm of the "imaginary" that is created in play (Vygotsky, 1976).

It may be because of its liminal quality that play creates opportunities for children (and adults) to imagine something beyond their given existence, a realm where they can be, according to Vygotsky's wonderful metaphor, "a head taller" than themselves. Today, most researchers of play in early childhood agree with Vygotsky's view that

> . . . play creates *a zone of proximal development* of the child. In play a child always behaves beyond his average age, above his daily behavior; in play, it is as though he were a head taller than himself. As in the focus of a magnifying glass, the play contains all developmental tendencies in a condensed form and is itself a major source of development" (Vygotsky, 1978, p. 102).

Vygotsky's concept of the "zone of proximal development" (ZPD) became well-known in contemporary Western developmental psychology. Only not for its connection to play but for its connection to education and learning. What has been less studied, despite being widely accepted, are the significant aspects of the "zone of proximal development" that originate in play and playful relationships among the participants. For instance, according to Peter Gray, a playful state of mind may be a necessary condition for many kinds of learning. Gray described numerous studies that " . . . show that learning, problem-solving, and creativity are worsened by interventions that interfere with playfulness and improved by interventions that promote playfulness" (Gray, 2013, p. 133). It seems that some kinds of play may create a specific quality in the relationships that are related to a free and leisurely, joint or solitary meaning-making (Beresin, 2010), and the players experience a sense of freedom. Thus, play may have a significant role in the development of self-reliance, self-efficacy, and self-determination (Stetsenko & Ho, 2015), as well as the authorial agency (Matusov, 2020; Rainio & Marjanovic-Shane, 2013). To play means to do something that has significance for the player and that can emotionally move them and their companions (Sutton-Smith et al., 2017).

Secondly, play seems to be deeply intertwined with the development of human "symbolic function," our ability to create and acquire a symbolic system of communication such as language and visual, musical, and gestural symbols (Vygotsky, 1976). In that sense, play is connected to human symbolic communication, which depends on the ability to create a layer of meta-communication (communication about communication) (Bateson, 1976).

Of course, there are many other lenses through which play can be understood, sometimes even in contradictory ways (Sutton-Smith, 1997), all related to some essential aspects of being human. For instance, I was just describing play through its developmental aspect, seeing play through the lens of progress. But play can be seen as fate (like in playing with chance and luck, gambling, etc.); play as testing power (sports, contests); play as identity (tradition, rituals, ceremonies, etc.); play as imaginary (related to imagination, flexibility, and creativity); play as an aesthetic experience in development of the self; etc. (Sutton-Smith, 1997). These different analytic lenses are not exclusionary. On the contrary, they are complimentary. Play, playfulness, and creativity may be that much more important and central to the richness of human experiences, cultures, and relationships.

Over the years of my studies, I have come to look at human play and playfulness as the distinctive way the players relate to the world, others, and the self. Play and playfulness depend on a few conditions. So far, I found that the following conditions and qualities seem to be necessary for play and playfulness to emerge:

a. Intrinsic significance—a play activity is about something that, first of all, matters *to the players* for reasons of their own.

b. Voluntary and owned by the players—A degree of freedom players have to voluntarily join or leave the playful activity and relate to others freely. "A key characteristic of play for children is that it is chosen and directed by the children themselves" (Gray, 2022). In other words, when participation in play is not voluntary but by some pressure or force, participants may not experience playfulness in the activity. Play is not play if a player does not own it.

c. Negotiated activity—when not solitary, playing relies on negotiations of the internal meanings and sense, power, and fairness among the players. These negotiations are a part of playing. They create a meta-level in the players' relationships. In other words, play may test the ethical aspect of the relationships among the players: how they treat others and how they feel they are treated. Or play may be about negotiating alternative ways of being and doing and making sense of these alternative perspectives. In addition, these negotiations create a meta-level in the players' relationships to a "referenced" reality—actual aspects of children's lives that play may be addressing.

d. Creativity in the (co)-authorship—Playing may probe the players' creativity in (co)authoring play moves. What does it mean to potentially come up with novel, surprising, powerful, and aesthetically appealing situations, plots, and twists? What counts as a "good" or even an "excellent" play move? Based on what values, principles, and/or aesthetics? (cf. John-Steiner, 2000).

Thus, I argue that play and playfulness seem to be specific ways of relating to the world, others, and self by way of an activity that is at once voluntary, purposeful, and deliberate practice of novel meaning-making. The players may experience it as attractive, joyful, and entertaining, but also as unpredictable, dramatic, suspenseful, and even tense both in its content (what the play is about) and in the negotiations among the players, testing their ideas, desires, powers, the strength of character, steadfastness, endurance, or flexibility, and creativity. Play is not always "happy, happy, joy, joy." It can be painful, risky and dramatic, too. It deals with all kinds of feelings, emotions, meanings, values, and ethics in relationships (Sutton-Smith et al., 2017). But it does it in ways that are deliberate, purposeful, intrinsically motivated, with heightened alertness that is moving for the players.

Although this approach to play is formed on the basis of many international studies, I think that these general assumptions about play still need to be further examined in diverse cultures and communities. As scholars of play, we should not rely only on our, to a great degree, unified points of view, which are chiefly developed in our Western philosophical outlook and mostly inspired by the Enlightenment. In fact, it might not always be easy to determine what counts as play, playfulness, and creativity, and especially what these concepts and the corresponding practices might mean in the lives of children in different cultures—or if they even exist (Rogoff, 2003; Sutton-Smith, 1972, 1976a, 1995).

Nevertheless, if we accept the general assumptions about play, playfulness, and creativity I described above, it is easy to see tensions between play, playfulness, and creativity, on the one hand, and the contemporary practices and policies of public education (on all levels), on the other.

TENSIONS BETWEEN CONVENTIONAL SCHOOLING AND PLAY, PLAYFULNESS AND CREATIVITY

To better understand these tensions, it is useful to situate public education in the social, cultural, and historical context. Public education in general, and especially early childhood education and care (ECEC), need to be seen as defined by the response to the changing role of families in raising their children and caring for them in modern industrial society. Before the advent of the Industrial Revolution, children's upbringing and education had been integral to the social, cultural, and economic lives of families and communities. Children's lives and upbringing were not separate spheres of knowledge or separate kinds of practice. But with the advent of the industrial-technological society, children were segregated from the social-economic lives of the adults, and child upbringing, care, and education were displaced from the family and close community lives. The practices of upbringing, education, and care became transformed and regulated by the economic and pedagogical-psychological models of the intervention (Marjanović, 1987b). The organizational aspects of the new ecology of children's lives were created as responses to the necessities of economic production, the organization of labor, the new mechanized, unified pace of time (Anderson, 1991), sorting by age as a normative tool, and hierarchical, meritocratic competition combined by the survival of the fittest among peers (Labaree, 2022). These ecological characteristics were manufactured for organizing children's lives, now decontextualized from the life of their communities and envisioned strictly as "preparation for life." Various solutions to that ecology have been driven by the ideology, principles, and values of new economic relationships and by the nascent philosophical, sociological, psychological, and pedagogical studies of childhood and child development. Without going deeper into the development of pedagogical theories and practices in early childhood upbringing and education, I think it is important to stress that the most significant change for children has been the fact that instead of living integrated into their family and community life and culture, their childhood now became an object of scientific study and their lives and subjectivities became objects of pedagogical processing (Marjanović, 1987b, 1987c). Play, playfulness, and creativity have been suppressed and excluded from publicly organized education (cf., Montessori, 1912). To some degree, this happened inadvertently, as a result of the ecological and organizational planning of children's lives: segregation from the richness of the socio-economic aspects of life, segregation by age and gender, decontextualization from public spheres of cultural and historical traditions, beliefs, and lore. But to a large degree, this suppression results from the tensions between the concepts of education and play and the understanding of their purpose and value in life.

- Where play needs to be an intrinsically significant activity for the child, the current conventional understanding of education and upbringing has been based on foisting preplanned activities on all children equally without taking their interests into account.
- Where play depends on the players' mutual voluntarism and their inalienable freedom to join or leave an activity, contemporary public education, even public early childhood education, are predominantly obligatory activities in which freedom to join or leave is almost completely erased.
- Where play includes negotiation of the meaning, power, and fairness among the participants, creating the meta-levels of communication (communication about communication) and reflection, public education is founded on an inalienable authority of the teacher/caregiver that

cannot be negotiated, and preset educational end-points and truths that cannot be questioned.

- Where play entails unpredictability, creativity, surprise, risk, and dramatic and aesthetical appeal, public education is based on known, pre-planned goals and endpoints. Surprise, risk, drama, creativity, or aesthetics are rarely appreciated, mostly seen as disruptive, and often actively suppressed.

The question for the planners of public educational policies then becomes a question of exploring these tensions and the boundaries between play, playfulness, and creativity on the one hand and various aspects of public education and upbringing on the other. For instance, is it possible to reduce the above-described tensions or even completely eliminate them? If so, how? What would be changed, and would these changes be good? Good for whom? Under what circumstances and in what local cultures? Who would benefit? Who would suffer, and in what ways? What would be the obstacles to such changes? What aspects of play, playfulness, and creativity could be incorporated into public education but not subordinated to it? Could education and upbringing become more intrinsic to the students? More voluntary for the students? More negotiated between the students and their educators? More unpredictable and surprising? More owned by the students? Could schooling incorporate more collaboration between the students and teachers as partners in and co-authors of various activities and practices?

VISIONS OF PUBLIC EDUCATION THAT SUPPORTS AND PROMOTES PLAY, PLAYFULNESS, AND CREATIVITY

In response to the current conditions of children's lives and growing up, public education and care, being purposeful and planned practices, do not necessarily have to be alienating, foisted, non-negotiable, and suppressing the unpredictability of human authorial agency. Indeed, the fact that education and upbringing ceased to be spontaneous by-products of communal living and became purposeful practices creates new social conditions where children and youth could be freed to develop in rich learning environments. That new freedom could open incredible opportunities to design a different ecology of life—an ecology supporting and promoting human dignity, self-actualization, self-determination, and critical and creative activities like play and playfulness. In such an ecology created for upbringing and education, children and youth could develop critical and creative examination of their relationships with the world, others, and self.

A new ecology of education as a "leisure" (Matusov, 2020) or education as a "scaled-down society" (Rietmulder, 2019), rather than the contemporary ecology of education as "labor," may create rich opportunities for transforming the boundaries between education and play, two distinct practices with their own separate territories and their own spheres. Education as a leisure or education as a scaled-down society could provide the possibility to incorporate diverse kinds of relationships, friendships, partnerships, hanging out with friends, personal interests and hobbies, etc. It could become a rich environment for all kinds of activities, which are neither play nor education in the traditional sense but could potentially be in synergy and lead to serendipitous events that can be both play and education.

Today, the ecology of public education still suppresses play, playfulness, and creativity. However, despite the domination of the conventional public school approach, there exist schools where play, playfulness, and creativity are not suppressed or excluded. On the contrary, in these schools, play and playfulness can flourish because students of all ages between 4 and 18 have the freedom to engage in activities voluntary, based on their interests, passions, and friendship across generations and genders, to negotiate with others what to do and how to organize their lives. They are free to imagine ways of being beyond the limitations of the given moment and organize exciting, unpredictable, and engaging projects, games, art, and studies. These schools are known as democratic schools, where the primary objective is not "learning" but "practicing life" (Rietmulder, 2019). Without going into a detailed description of democratic schools, which is beyond the scope of this "play manifesto," I want to conclude by quoting a recent alumnus of a democratic school whom I interviewed a few weeks before his graduation. This is what he told me: "When I originally came to this school in the fifth grade, I first 'fell asleep' for about six months. But then, I woke up and started to live."

NOTE

1. In Greece, public education is mandatory from the age of 4 years old. See https://eurydice.eacea.ec.europa.eu/national-education-systems/greece/early-childhood-education-and-care#:~:text=Compulsory%20pre%2Dschool%20education%20in,(Law%204704%2F2020).

REFERENCES

Anderson, B. (1991). *Imagined communities: Reflections on the origin and spread of nationalism* (Rev. and extended ed.). Verso.

Bateson, G. (1976). A Theory of Play and Fantasy. In J. S. Bruner, A. Jolly, & K. Sylva (Eds.), *Play: Its Role in Development and Evolution* (pp. 119–129). Penguin Books.

Beresin, A. (2010). *Recess Battles: Playing, Fighting and Storytelling*. The University Press of Mississippi.

Bronfenbrenner, U. (1981). *The Ecology of Human Development*. Harvard University Press.

Brown, F., & Patte, M. (2013). *Rethinking children's play*. Bloomsbury Academic.

Brown, F., & Taylor, C. (Eds.). (2008). *Foundations of Playwork*. Open University Press.

Brown, F., & Webb, S. (2008). Children without play: a research project. In F. Brown & C. Taylor (Eds.), *Foundations of Playwork* (pp. 274–277). Open University Press.

Bruner, J. S. (1968). *Toward a theory of instruction*. Norton.

Bruner, J. S. (1976). Nature and Uses of Immaturity. In J. S. Bruner, A. Jolly, & K. Sylva (Eds.), *Play: Its Role in Development and Evolution* (pp. 28 — 64). Penguin Books.

Bruner, J. S., Jolly, A., & Sylva, K. (1976). *Play: its role in development and evolution*. Basic Books.

Bruner, J. S., & Sherwood. (1976). Peekaboo and the Learning of Rule Structures. In J. S. Bruner, A. Jolly, & K. Sylva (Eds.), *Play—Its Role in Development and Evolution*. Penguin Books, Ltd.

Burghardt, G. M. (2005). *The genesis of animal play: testing the limits*. MIT Press.

Calhoun, C. J. (1992). *Habermas and the public sphere*. MIT press.

Elmore, R. F., & Fuhrman, S. (1990). The National Interest and the Federal Role in Education. *Publius*, *20*(3), 149–162. http://www.jstor.org/stable/3330220

Gladwin, M. (2008). The Concept of Risk in Play and Playwork. In F. Brown & C. Taylor (Eds.), *Foundations of Playwork*. Open University Press.

Graeber, D., & Wengrow, D. (2021). *The dawn of everything: a new history of humanity* (First American edition. ed.). Farrar, Straus and Giroux.

Gray, P. (2010). The decline of play and rise in children's mental disorders. *Psychology Today*, *26*.

Gray, P. (2013). *Free to learn: why unleashing the instinct to play will make our children happier, more self-reliant, and better students for life*. Basic Books.

Gray, P. (2022, May 15, 2022). What Is Play? How Children Define It. *Psychology Today*. https://www.psychologytoday.com/us/blog/freedom-learn/202205/what-is-play-how-children-define-it

Gripsrud, J., & Eide, M. (2010). *The idea of the public sphere: a reader*. Lexington Books.

Holloway, S. L., & Pimlott-Wilson, H. (2014). Enriching children, institutionalizing childhood? Geographies of play, extracurricular activities, and parenting in England. *Annals of the Association of American Geographers*, *104*(3), 613–627.

Huizinga, J. (2009). *Homo ludens: A study of the play-element in culture*. Routledge.

John-Steiner, V. (2000). *Creative collaboration*. Oxford University Press.

Labaree, D. F. (2022, 2022/12/22). School Gave Me the Creeps. *David Labaree on Schooling, History and Writing*. https://davidlabaree.com/2022/12/22/school-gave-me-the-creeps-2/

Lareau, A. (2003). *Unequal childhoods: class, race, and family life*. University of California Press.

London, R. A. (2019). The right to play: Eliminating the opportunity gap in elementary school recess. *Phi Delta Kappan, 101*(3), 48–52.

Marjanović, S. (1977). *Dečja igra i stvaralaštvo [Children's Play and Creativity]* (Vol. 70). Prosvetni Pregled.

Marjanović, S. (1979). Stvaralaštvo, igra i vaspitanje [Creativity, Play and Education]. *Predskolsko Dete, 9*(1–2), 1–15.

Marjanović, S. (1987a). Dečja igra i stvaralaštvo [Child Play and Creativity]. *Predskolsko Dete, 17*(1–4), 85–101.

Marjanović, S. (1987b). Kritika institucionalizacije predskolskog obrazivanja i teze za nacrt koncepcije društvenog obrazovanja kao otvorenog sistema [A critique of the institutionalization of early childhood education and an initial conceptualization of societal education as an open system]. *Predskolsko Dete, 17*(1–4), 403–411.

Marjanović, S. (1987c). Protivrečna pitanja javnog obrazovanja predskolske dece [The controversial issues in public education of pre/school children]. *Predskolsko Dete, 1987*(1–4), 11–26.

Matusov, E. (2020). *Envisioning education in a post-work leisure-based society: A dialogic perspective*. Palgrave. https://doi.org/10.1007/978-3-030-46373-1

Matusov, E., Marjanovic-Shane, A., & Meacham, S. (2016). Pedagogical voyeurism: Dialogic critique of documentation and assessment of learning. *International Joournal of European Psychology*, 1–26. https://doi.org/http://dx.doi.org/10.1080/21594937.2014.931686

McKendrick, J. H., Bradford, M. G., & Fielder, A. V. (2000). Kid customer? Commercialization of playspace and the commodification of childhood. *Childhood, 7*(3), 295–314.

Montessori, M. (1912). *The Montessori Method*. Frederick A. Stokes Company.

Opie, I. A., & Opie, P. (1967). *The lore and language of school-children*. Clarendon P.

Opie, I. A., & Opie, P. (1969). *Children's games in street and playground: chasing, catching, seeking, hunting, racing, duelling, exerting, daring, guessing, acting, pretending*. Clarendon Press.

Patte, M. (2009). The State of Recess in Pennsylvania Elementary Schools: A Continuing Tradition or a Distant Memory? In C. Clark (Ed.), *Transactions at Play* (pp. 147–165). University Press of America, Inc.

Pellegrini, A. D. (2008). The Recess Debate: A Discjuncture between Educational Policy and Scientific Research. *American Journal of Play, 1*(2), 181–191.

Piaget, J. (1951). *Play, dreams and imitation in childhood*. Norton.

Propp, V. I. A., Liberman, A., & ebrary, I. (1984). *Theory and history of folklore*. University of Minnesota Press. http://site.ebrary.com/lib/ucsc/Doc?id=10151076http://site.ebrary.com/lib/ucmerced/Doc?id=10151076

Rainio, A. P., & Marjanovic-Shane, A. (2013). From ambivalence to agency: Becoming an author, an actor and a hero in a drama workshop. *Learning, Culture and Social Interaction, 2*(2), 111–125. https://doi.org/10.1016/j.lcsi.2013.04.001

Ramstetter, C., & Murray, R. (2017). Time to Play: Recognizing the Benefits of Recess. *American Educator, 41*(1), 17.

Riesman, D., Glazer, N., & Denney, R. (1961). *The lonely crowd: a study of the changing American character.* Yale University Press.

Rietmulder, J. (2019). *When kids rule the school: The power and promise of democratic education.* New Society Publishers.

Rinaldi, C. (1998). Projected Curriculum Constructed Through Documentation—Progettazione: An Interview with Leila Gandini. In C. Edwards, L. Gandini, & G. Forman (Eds.), *The Hundred Languages of Children, The Reggio Emilia Approach—Advanced Reflections* (pp. 113–125). Ablex Publishing Corporation.

Rogoff, B. (1990). *Apprenticeship in thinking: cognitive development in social context.* Oxford University Press.

Rogoff, B. (2003). *The Cultural nature of Human Development.* Oxford University Press.

Schieffelin, B. B., & Ochs, E. (Eds.). (1979). *Developmental Pragmatics.* Academic Press.

Schieffelin, B. B., & Ochs, E. (1986). *Language socialization across cultures.* Cambridge University Press.

Stetsenko, A. P., & Ho, P.-C. G. (2015). The Serious Joy and the Joyful Work of Play: Children Becoming Agentive Actors in Co-Authoring Themselves and Their World Through Play. *International Journal of Early Childhood,* 1–14.

Striniste, N. A., & Moore, R. C. (1989). Early childhood outdoors: A literature review related to the design of childcare environments. *Children's Environments Quarterly,* 25–31.

Sutton-Smith, B. (1972). *The folkgames of children.* Published for the American Folklore Society by the University of Texas Press.

Sutton-Smith, B. (1973). *Child psychology.* Appleton-Century-Crofts.

Sutton-Smith, B. (1976a). *A Children's games anthology: studies in folklore and anthropology.* Arno Press.

Sutton-Smith, B. (1976b). *The Psychology of play.* Arno Press.

Sutton-Smith, B. (1981). *The folkstories of children.* University of Pennsylvania Press.

Sutton-Smith, B. (1995). *Childrens' folklore: a source book.* Garland.

Sutton-Smith, B. (1997). *The ambiguity of play.* Harvard University Press.

Sutton-Smith, B., Phillips, C. L., Adams, G. R., Eberle, S. G., & Hogan, P. (2017). *Play for Life: Play Theory and Play as Emotional Survival.* The Strong. https://books.google.com/books?id=iaL5MAAACAAJ

Taylor, C. (2008). Playwork and theory of Loose parts. In F. Brown & C. Taylor (Eds.), *Foundations of Playwork* (pp. 44–47). Open University Press.

Turner, V. W. (1982). *From ritual to theatre: the human seriousness of play.* Performing Arts Journal Publications.

Vygotsky, L. S. (1976). Play and its role in the mental development of the child. In J. S. Bruner, A. Jolly, & K. Sylva (Eds.), *Play—Its Role in Development and Evolution* (pp. 537–554). Penguin Books, Ltd. (1933)

Vygotsky, L. S. (1978). The Role of Play in Development. In M. Cole, V. John-Steiner, S. Scribner, & E. Souberman (Eds.), *Mind in Society: The Development of Higher Psychological Processes* (pp. 93–104). Harvard University Press.

Vygotsky, L. S. (1987). Imagination and its development in childhood (N. Minick, Trans.). In R. W. Rieber & A. S. Carton (Eds.), *The collected works of L.S. Vygotsky* (Vol. 1, pp. 339–350). Plenum Press.

Vygotsky, L. S. (1998). Imagination and creativity in adolescent (M. J. Hall, Trans.). In R. W. Rieber & J. Wollock (Eds.), *The collected works of L. S. Vygotsky* (Vol. 5, pp. 151–166). Plenum Press. (Original work published in Pedologija podrostka, Moscow: Izd-vo BZO pri Pedfake 2-go MGU, 1931)

Chapter 7

The Ambiguity of Love

A Commedia dell'arte Scenario Based on the Seven Rhetorics of Play of Brian Sutton-Smith's Famous Work (with scholarly commentary)

John Joseph Cash and John A. Cross

Commedia dell'arte is a European traditional and improvisational form of stage performance originating in mid-1500s Italy. It can be traced by its written sources, the scenaria (or scripts), and by the introduction of its characters into European performance traditions including Shakespeare, opera, Punch-and-Judy, pantomime, vaudeville, post-fascist Italian street theater, and contemporary sit-coms.

Unlike most modern Western theater, the words of the script are not the creative heart of a commedia performance. A scenario simply provides directions to the actors for what must take place on stage and move things along. The directions can be quite brief, as "They argue." Rather, the characters are at the heart. They catch at their audiences' sense of amusement and underlying truth. Commedia was originally improvisational, which was rendered permanent by text and script. The potential it had was reclaimed in the post-World War II era (Crick 2018). This allows, to paraphrase Alberto Naselli (stage name Zan Ganassa, commedia performer of the 1500s) in his famous prologues, for commedia to develop in the actor a facility for observing interactions in life. Presenting these on stage, every succeeding performance will develop a successively deeper understanding of the interactions represented. It is by inhabiting the role over many performances that the commedia actor creates the role (Ojeda Calvo, 2007).

Our seven commedia characters are representative of the characters found in early commedia plays. As commedia developed in the 17th and 18th century hundreds more were created. They are stereotype or stock characters, but they are not mere stereotypes, nor allegorical figures; they represent aspects of human experience.

Venues for commedia dell'arte performances today include the many living history events with a medieval or Renaissance themes. Cash and Cross have both performed commedia at events run by the Society for Creative Anachronism (SCA); Cross' troupe is a regular at the SCA's annual Pennsic War. It might be worth a few sentences to go quickly into the role of play in living history.

The Society for Creative Anachronism, according to its website, is "an inclusive community pursuing research and re-creation of pre-seventeenth century skills, arts, combat and culture. The lives of participants are enriched as we gain knowledge of history through activities, demonstrations, and events." It claims today to have over 10,000 members worldwide. Its historical focus is the European Middle Ages, and its cultural focus is on chivalry (or martial prowess and sportsmanlike respect) as it is imagined to have existed as an ideal in those days.

Living history, both as social and as professional museum education, involves these elements: (1) Performative presentation or representation, (2) The making or purchase of historically accurate material culture (such as dress, equipment, or weapons) and its subsequent display in the performance, (3) Accuracy or authenticity of material culture and behavior, in so far as these contribute to a desirable simulation of a chosen historical period, (4) The relationship of performer and display of authenticity with audiences to whom the performance is directed (self, private, public, the honored dead) as well as with performance venues (private or public), (5) The practical and social organization of a living history group (its size, choice of period and level of authenticity, its educational or other purposes, its relationship with venues) (Erisman 1998; Cash 2003).

It should be clear that living history offers many opportunities for play, predominantly, but by no means exclusively, among adults. In particular, the centrality of honorable combat, whether represented at Gettysburg or at Hastings, serves living history groups as a cultural focus, to the extent that the conceptual (and often physical) center of an event is a tournament or battle, which gives pride of place to the rhetoric of power in understanding such historical recreations as contests between players or teams. But the artifact of material culture, often hand-made, and necessary to make the recreation historic, even authentic, can carry symbolic weight. A beautifully made gown commands attention just as a well-forged sword does. More importantly for us, both are toys with which participants play.

Commedia performances, like plays and concerts, act as relaxation for audiences after a day of recreating. Here the performers in the recreation can let others take over that job. There's something of the touristic in this: audience members for the event can participate or immerse themselves to various degrees, for reasons that go range from the personal to the intensely communal, they can purchase souvenirs and take selfies, and under certain circumstances they can become the objects of other people's touristic gaze (Kirschenblatt-Gimblett and Bruner, 300–307; Urry, esp. 4–5).

Sutton-Smith's rhetorics, though addressed individually in his chapters, in fact emerge from the interplay of factors, which are signified by ambiguities perceived by both players and scholars. Cross has composed a commedia scenario in which each of the characters represents some aspect of the seven rhetorics of play listed by Sutton-Smith, while still adhering to the examples typical of a sixteenth century commedia dell'arte scenario. It has been prepared this for performance as though some group of actors might someday try to present it.

What might we learn from placing the rhetorics in interaction or opposition as a play, in fact a commedia? It is curious how each of the rhetorics of play adapt to being acted out by the traditional characters. These rhetorics emerge from the interplay of factors, which are signified by ambiguities perceived by both players and scholars. As the plot unfolds and the characters interact, the rhetorics interact as well. Cash has added notes to the scenario to highlight these interactions.

AMBIGUITY OF LOVE

Ambiguità dell'amore 6M-3F

Table 7.1. Dramatis Personae and Props

Dramatis Personae		*Props*
Magnifico	Wealthy merchant—Fate	Musical instrument
Isabella	Magnifico's daughter—Imaginary	Book
Mezzatino	Magnifico's servant—Self	A marriage contract
Franceschina	Isabella's nurse—Identity	A deck of cards
Orazio	Fabbrodelsud's son—Progress	A small empty sack
Capitano Arroganzo	A Soldier—Power	Mezzatino's collection
Zani	Arroganzo's servant—Frivolity	
Dottore Fabbrodelsud	A scholar	Set: Two Houses

Special Skills and Effects

Orazio should have some musical or dancing talent that he shows progress with during the play.
Zani should be adept at handling playing cards.

Performance Considerations

This play is intended to highlight the teachings of Brian Sutton-Smith, and the actors playing it should be at least mildly versed in his book "The Ambiguity of Play." The character playing Dottore Fabbrodelsud most of all, perhaps having some excerpts memorized, or at least well paraphrased.

Backstory (Argomento)

In the city of Mantua, Magnifico and Dottore Fabbrodelsud have been neighbors for a long time. Their children, Isabella and Orazio, have been growing in affection for each other. Magnifico is a gambler, both in business and with cards. Recently, while on business trip to Napoli, he resolved his losses in a dubious card game by agreeing to give his daughter in marriage to a Spanish Capitano. He kept this embarrassing loss a secret on his return.

Act I

Table 7.2. Act I

1.01	**Isabella**	Isabella monologues a fantasy in which she is the lady in a romance story, swept up in love by her wonderful Orazio.[1] She is interrupted.
1.02	**Magnifico**	Magnifico tells Isabella that she must stop seeing that foolish musician Orazio. He wants her to marry a man with influence, and who can help his business grow.[2] They argue in a lazzo of accusing the other of not understanding the rules.[3] Isabella loses. Crying, **Isabella withdraws**. Magnifico calls Mezzatino.
1.03	**Mezzatino**	Mezzatino dutifully responds. Magnifico tells him to keep Isabella from spending time with Orazio. Mezzatino agrees. **Magnifico exits** up the street. Mezzatino complains that he was interrupted from working on his collection (*could be anything inexpensive, e.g. collection of plum pits that look like famous play theorists*).

1.04 **Franceschina**	Franceschina is furious that someone has made Isabella sob uncontrollably. She blames Mezzatino. Mezzatino says that their master has told him to keep Orazio away from Isabella.[4] Franceschina does a short song or dance lazzo about the ways of their people.
1.05 **Orazio**	Orazio looks to Isabella's balcony. Mezzatino tells him to go home. Franceschina shows him some sympathy. **Mezzatino and Franceschina exit into Magnifico's house.**
	Orazio begins playing music, while monologuing about his love for Isabella, and how he needs to get so good at playing his music that no one would refuse to let her marry him. He begins sobbing.[5]
1.06 **Dottore Fabbrodelsud**	After a lazzo about the quality of Orazio's music, Fabbrodelsud asks his son why he is crying. Orazio tells him that he does not know why, but suddenly Magnifico doesn't want him to see Isabella. Fabbrodelsud tells Orazio to practice indoors. **Orazio exits** into Fabbrodelsud's house.
	Fabbrodelsud monologues speculating that Magnifico is playing some kind of game.[6]
1.07 **Capitano Arroganzo Zani**	Arroganzo demands to know where Magnifico lives. Zani asides that this neighborhood's peaceful look is an affront to the turmoil of the human condition. Fabbrodelsud is oblivious to Arroganzo's threatening qualities which aggravates Arroganzo.[7] Fabbrodelsud goes with them to Magnifico's door and knocks.[8]
1.08 **Franceschina Mezzatino**	They ask Arroganzo what he wants. He demands to see Magnifico and Magnifico's beautiful daughter.[9]
1.09 **Magnifico**	Magnifico tells Arroganzo that he has come too soon. He should go to the Inn and come back in an hour when the fates say he will be more welcome. After some back-and-forth, **Arroganzo and Zani exit** up the street.[10]
	Magnifico gestures and Mezzatino follows them. **Mezzatino exits.**
	Magnifico calls Isabella.
1.10 **Isabella**	Magnifico tells her to get cleaned up and dressed, because she will be married in an hour. Isabella is delighted. Franceschina tells her that it isn't to Orazio. Isabella is devastated. Fabbrodelsud asks how this came to pass. Magnifico confesses that he lost her playing Primero. Everyone argues and fights. **Everyone exits.**[11]

Act II

2.01	**Isabella** **Franceschina**	Isabella sobs that this is like the upsetting parts of her romance stories. Franceschina complains that the Capitano isn't one of us, and probably can't sing any of the songs or do any of the dances.[12]
2.02	**Orazio**	Orazio plays a sad song and says loving things to Isabella. Franceschina tells him to go home. He is just making it worse. He attempts to go, but Isabella begs him to stay. **Franceschina withdraws.** Orazio continues wooing Isabella.
2.03	**Mezzatino**	Mezzatino tells the couple to hide. Arroganzo is coming now. **Orazio hides** to observe. **Isabella withdraws.**
2.04	**Franceschina**	Franceschina tells Mezzatino that foreigners like the Capitano shouldn't marry our maidens. Mezzatino agrees.
2.05	**Capitano** **Arroganzo** **Zani**	Arroganzo demands to see Magnifico. Zani looks at Mezzatino and then shows his desire for Franceschina. Mezzatino calls for Magnifico. Franceschina tries to keep Zani at arm's length. Arroganzo tells Zani to behave better in front of the ladies.
2.06	**Magnifico**	Magnifico tells Franceschina to go inside and bring out a small table with food and drink. **Franceschina exits** into the house. Magnifico tells Arroganzo to be patient, as Isabella is getting ready. Zani sees Orazio and waves him on. **Orazio steps forward.** Zani proposes that they play Primero to pass the time.
2.07	**Dottore** **Fabbrodelsud**	Fabbrodelsud hears about Primero and wants to watch. Magnifico and Mezzatino also agree to play for low stakes.
2.08	**Franceschina**	Zani produces a deck and shuffles it, while Orazio, Mezzatino, and Magnifico get ready to play. Arroganzo speaks his internal monologue about how his new bride will see that she is the luckiest woman to get such a husband. **Franceschina exits to help Isabella.** In a lazzo, the card game gets animated as Zani keeps winning.
2.09	**Isabella** **Franceschina**	[Isabella is nicely dressed but sobbing] Isabella talks living the sad part of a romance story. Arroganzo tells tales of his many exploits to prove his worth. Mezzatino is sure he is going to win this hand and bets his collection (*see scene 1.03*). Orazio is furious at his luck. Zani wins again. Zani puts his winnings in a sack.

| 2.10 | Arroganzo declares the game over. He says the time for the wedding is now! Fabbrodelsud asks to see the marriage contract. After examining it, Fabbrodelsud says that another hour is needed to adhere to all local protocols. Taking the contract, **Arroganzo and Zani exit** up the street. Furious about their losses, **Mezzatino, Magnifico, and Orazio exit** into their houses.[13] Isabella says that Orazio will save her. Franceschina admires Arroganzo. **Isabella and Franceschina exit** into the house. |

Act III

Table 7.4. Act III

3.01	**Mezzatino** **Dottore** **Fabbrodelsud**	Mezzatino is upset about losing his collection. Fabbrodelsud tells him that Zani's game was not fair, and that if someone accepts breaking one rule in one game then when with that person all rules of all games are subject to corruption. He hopes Mezzatino can get the collection back. **Fabbrodelsud exits into his house.** Mezzatino calls Franceschina.
3.02	**Franceschina**	Franceschina practices a traditional wedding dance. Mezzatino tells her that he has a plan to help Isabella and Orazio, but he needs her help. She agrees. **Franceschina and Mezzatino exit** up the street.
3.03	**Orazio** **Isabella**	Orazio does a good job playing an inspiring love song.[14] Isabella loves how this fits her story. Isabella says that they have to find a way to escape and marry.
3.04	**Magnifico**	Magnifico hears the end of the story, and says that honor demands that she go with Arroganzo. Orazio declares that Primero was just a game, but marriage is life. Magnifico defends the honor of following the fate dictated by the game.[15]
3.05	**Capitano** **Arroganzo** **Zani**	Arroganzo declares that he has waited long enough, and now is the time to celebrate this wedding. He is interrupted.
3.06	**Mezzatino** **Franceschina**	Mezzatino offers Arroganzo double or nothing. In a game, if Arroganzo wins, he gets Franceschina as a wife for Arlecchino and a double wedding. If he loses, he gives up his claim on Isabella. Zani begs Arroganzo to agree, as they never lose. Arroganzo agrees. Mezzatino asks for Fabbrodelsud to be a judge of the fairness of the game. Arroganzo reluctantly agrees. They call Fabbrodelsud.

3.07	**Dottore Fabbrodelsud**	Fabbrodelsud agrees to be the judge. Mezzatino says that they must use a new deck of cards, which Fabbrodelsud will make sure aren't marked. Zani objects, saying his cards are perfect. Fabbrodelsud examines them and shows how they are unfairly cut and marked. He asks if these were the same cards used in Napoli to win Isabella. Zani furiously denies it. Arroganzo says yes, and then scolds Zani. Arroganzo asks how much of his luck over the last ten years was from cheating? Zani says all of it.[16]
3.08		Arroganzo faces Magnifico and tears up the contract. He looks to Isabella and says that she is a woman worthy of true love in whatever form of man that comes in. Franceschina praises Arroganzo's honor and begs him to take her with him. He agrees.[17] **Arroganzo, Zani, and Franceschina exit** up the street.
3.09		Orazio plays a short bit of music and asks Magnifico if he could marry Isabella. Magnifico says yes. Celebrating, **Orazio and Isabella exit** to record their marriage.[18]
3.10		Mezzatino, Magnifico, and Fabbrodelsud discuss games, rules, and the ambiguity of honor. **All exit**.

We conclude with some notes on honor, on toys, and on tourism.

Cross' scenario ends with a testament of honor which wins for both Orazio and Arroganzo their lady loves. Honor figures rarely in Sutton-Smith's rhetorics, but it peeps out at times, in particular in contests (rhetoric of power). Honor is a complex thing, say Peristiani and Pitt-Rivers. It is a special medium of social exchange; it has "a congenital relationship with grace," being a gift given regardless of merit (independent of the rhetoric of Progress, akin to that of Fate). It can inhabit tokens or artifacts, making them "vehicles of grace" circulating as in the well-known Kula ring. Honor reflects "the sacredness of power" (Peristiani and Pitt-Rivers, 3). In so far as play acts as a mediating behavior in sports, girding a competition with behaviors reinforcing honor in participation ameliorate the sting of defeat in Japan's national sport of sumo wrestling (Sutton-Smith, 77).

In its capacity as an honor-bearing token at also serves the function of a toy in play. Much written on living history has focused on authenticity of things made or produced, but not much on whether they carry honor or are sources of grace. This seems strange given the symbolism of weapons as symbols of power in contests around which the living history event's activities are ordered (Stoeltje 1993), and the role of the public sphere as a stage upon which one must elaborate personal honor so as to maintain grace (Pia di Bella, 164). The SCA centers on the performance of chivalry. This is on display with most consequence in combat, on the tourney field or in battles. A person pursuing a path from beginner fighter to knight and is the group's archetypal hero tale, of which songs and stories have been written (e.g. O'Donnell 2004). To the extent that toys are the material culture that presents to the SCA audience's gaze a realized medieval play-world, the most compelling toys are swords, armor, crowns.

A theatrical performance allows attendees at living history events to be tourists to their own performance. In so far as authenticity is concerned and supports the claims of the play-world to be other than the real world, attending a good performance of Shakespeare or commedia dell'arte puts one in an authentic center devoid of the tasks of chivalrous combat. What do such performances do for audiences already at play? We suggest they allow members of the play-world to act as tourists, sitting back and letting others do the work of authentic historical recreation. They play the way medieval people would have played. Thus the performance becomes in a sense an artifact—a toy, a souvenir for their tourist gaze, something for consumption. But an ephemeral artifact, like a tournament: "the ephemerality of historical performance, compounded by the doubly ephemeral practice of improvisation, puts commedia dell'arte in a place where methodology and mythology struggle for supremacy, and what is performed as commedia today has become a contested area." (Crick 2002).

NOTES

1. Isabella represents the rhetoric of the Imaginary. From here on the rhetoric represented will simply be stated, as "Imaginary confronts Power."

2. Orazio represents Progress. Why he figures being a musician will lead him to a fate-free future is hard to fathom. But he has plans. While Magnifico too has plans, he is in fact relying on luck to keep the family powerful. Venture capitalism is all about risk and luck. Orazio is about nothing of that sort. Responding to Magnifico (as Imagination to Fate), Isabella is striving to reconcile his ideal of the best outcome with the unity and diversity of her best outcome. Both understand the mutability of things. Like Lewis Carroll (Alice, the Knight and his song) Magnifico "has a competitive game mentality and shows how ambiguous this kind of play can be for Alice, although it is highly flexible and logical for the Knight" (Sutton-Smith, 138). Magnifico shows he is just as much a master of conflating art and play as Isabella. Ultimately, Magnifico behaves here as if, so far as life is a game, the game of life has rules. And cheating is allowed (and has its own rules).

3. A lazzo in commedia dell'arte is defined by the actors as "a piece of business." It is better understood to us as a shtick or a comic routine.

4. Franceschina represents Identity. Here, Identity casts blame and responsibility upon Self for upsetting Imagination. In a sense, the community has singled out a player for not playing nicely. Self explains that Fate, through its acquisition of Power,

has directed it (Self as player) to keep Imaginary from being influenced by Progress. But Identity doesn't buy Self's excuse.

5. The interaction of Isabella (Imaginary) and Orazio (Progress) epitomizes the distinction discussed in Sutton-Smith between play and art, or between bottom up play versus top-down logic. Youthful ardor aside, this relationship is not likely to work out well. Self as player attempts to influence Progress, as instructed by Fate. Identity sympathizes with Progress, and Identity and Self look to form a partnership.

6. Dottore Fabbrodelsud (whose identity should be apparent) asks Progress about its unhappiness. Progress sees its way blocked by Fate. Fate, speculates the Scholar, is playing a game involving Imagination and other rhetorics, not simply as ways they interact, but a specific game in which each might be a player—or someone else might be.

7. Arroganzo represents Power, Zani represents Frivolity. Power is aggravated by the Scholar's casual attitude. Power wonders, is the Scholar trying to subvert his power by playful inversion? Or perhaps appropriate it? (Power frequently wonders these things about Scholars).

8. The inverse of fate knocking at one's door is when two rhetorics and a play theorist knock on fate's door.

9. Identity and Self confront Power, an ancient rhetoric. Power in turn demands an encounter with Imagination, thus dealing with all three newer rhetorics.

10. Fate exerts dominance over Power. Power and Frivolity interact. Tripping up of order and making a mess of things ensues.

11. Fate commands Imagination. Imagination is delighted then devastated by Fate. Fate confesses its arbitrariness/capriciousness, even kinship with Frivolity. But all is not lost. For "what is difficult to grasp in The Decameron, Mazotta says, is that the ambiguity of play forms and their meanings is used to emphasize their precariousness and yet also their autonomy." (Sutton-Smith, 139). Isabella (rhetoric of imagination) is a piece still in play.

12. A person is not part of the play community if they don't know the rules of games

13. Either Fabbrodelsud must ensure adherence to local protocols, or he is doing a "windshield survey" and requires time to complete his grant application to the NEA to study this new-found community of play and players. A contract is essentially a list of rules by which players agree to abide. Cheating may be allowed, but not outright breach. Inviting Fabbrodelsud, father of Orazio (Progress), into a contract between Power and Fate is curiously reckless of these parties. It is interesting to compare the fury of the three characters here: Magnifico is furious that Fate let him down, while Mezzatino (Self) and Orazio (Progress), who see the world as ordered, are furious that their plans, practice, and good sportsmanship did not shift things in their favor.

14. Orazio (Progress) provides evidence of successful practice.

15. Here is one ambiguity: the ambiguity of sense (is this serious, or is it nonsense?) Orazio states the classic difference in the rhetoric of progress, that play is not serious but actual progress is. Also, honor is an important social construct in play, although Sutton-Smith does not mention it much. Magnifico suggests that even games of fate have rules that must be followed if one's honor is to be preserved.

16. Here we see the ambiguity of transition (you said you were only playing) – Zani reveals he has deluded Arroganzo into thinking his success was won honorably. But the issue of honor in play—of the players and of the game—is complex. Frivolity demonstrates how it has the real power over Power, supporting it in a subversive way all along while appearing to be mere frivolous play.

17. Power makes a sacrificial gesture to Fate, a gamble with it, even though both desire this set of rules to be valid. "One who plays with the ambiguity of his own pretense must ultimately be perceived as being at play in some form. Playing with just that ambiguity—whether he really means it or is just playing—is the most ambiguous form of play" (Sutton-Smith, 150).

18. Perhaps the power accrued to fate must make a gesture of grace to reinforce its role as source of power? Rhetoric of progress always seeks to document its evidence.

REFERENCES

Cash, John Joseph. Borrowed Time: Reenacting the American Civil War in Indiana. Doctoral dissertation, Indiana University, 2003.

Crick, Olly. "(Re) evaluating improvisation in commedia dell'arte." (Online journal) Comedy Studies, Vol. 13 issue 2 (2002): Comic Improv, pp. 125–138.

Crick, Olly. Approaching Aesthetic Positions for Neo☐Commedia (1946☐2016): A Dramaturgical Investigation, Mindful of the Potential for Local, Social and Political Relevance. Thesis, Edge Hill University, 2018.

Cross, John A. 40 Brilliant Comedies: Easily Played, Updated, Commedia dell'Arte Scenarios from Flaminio Scala's 1611 Collection "il Teatro delle Favole Rappresentative." Foreword by Olly Crick. Berlin MA: Truth and Beauty Media, 2022.

Erisman, Wendy. Forward into the past: The poetics and politics of community in two historical re-creation groups. Doctoral dissertation, University of Texas at Austin, 1998.

Kirschenblatt-Gimblett, Barbara, and Edward M. Bruner. "Tourism." In Folklore, Cultural Performances, and Popular Entertainments. A Communications-centered Handbook. Oxford university Press, 1992, pp. 300–307.

Mazzotta, Giuseppe. The world at play in Boccaccio's Decameron. Princeton, NJ.: Princeton University Press, 1986.

Patrick O'Donnell. The Knights Next Door: Everyday People Living Middle Ages Dreams. ʃiUniverse, 2004.

Peristiani, J.G. and Julian Pitt-Rivers, eds. Honor and Grace in Anthropology. Honor and Grace in Anthropology (Cambridge Studies in Social and Cultural Anthropology, Series Number 76). Cambridge: Cambridge University Press, 1992.

Ojeda Calvo, Maria Del Valle. Stefanelo Botarga e Zan Ganassa. Scenari e zibaldoni di comici italiani nella Spagna del Cinquecento (Vol. 1) (Biblioteca teatrale). Rome, 2007.

J.G. Peristiany and Julian Pitt-Rivers, eds. Honor and Grace in Anthropology (Cambridge Studies in Social and Cultural Anthropology, Series Number 76). Cambridge: Cambridge University Press, 1992.

Pia di Bella, Maria. "Name, blood, and miracles: the claims to renown in traditional Sicily." The Future of Play Theory. A Multidisciplinary Inquiry into the Contributions of Brian Sutton-Smith. Anthony D. Pellegrini, editor. Albany: State University of New York Press, 1995, pp. 151–166.

Stoeltje, Beverly J. "Power and the Ritual Genres: American Rodeo." Western Folklore Vol. 52 No. 2/4 (Apr-Oct. 1993), pp. 135–156.

Sutton-Smith, Brian. The Ambiguity of Play. Cambridge, Harvard University Press, 1998.

Urry, John. The Tourist Gaze: Leisure and Travel in Contemporary Societies (Published in association with Theory, Culture & Society). SAGE Publications Ltd., 2003 (1990).

Chapter 8

From the Streets of Wellington to the Ivy League: Reflecting on a Lifetime of Play

An Interview with Brian Sutton-Smith

Conducted by Fraser Brown and Michael Patte

This interview came about because Brian Sutton-Smith was invited to deliver a keynote address at the 50th Anniversary International Play Association (IPA) Conference in Cardiff, Wales, but due to failing health, he was unable to attend. The conference organizers were keen to have input from Brian and delegated Fraser Brown to conduct an interview during the 2011 conference of The Association for the Study of Play (TASP). In collaboration with Michael Patte, the President of TASP, questions were framed for the interview and shared with Brian in advance. However, those who know Brian will not be surprised to hear that on the day of the interview he simply checked that the camera was rolling, and then started talking. He stopped about an hour later, having delivered a presentation of the highest quality. Those who were present felt privileged to have been there.

The interview took place in the *Brian Sutton-Smith Library and Archives of Play*, at the Strong National Museum of Play, on April 29th, 2011. An edited DVD of the interview was shown at the IPA Conference on Thursday July 7th, 2011. The interview appeared in full in the first Issue of the *International*

Journal of Play, and is reproduced here with the permission of the publishers, Taylor & Francis.

* * *

Question: Would you like to start by sharing some of your memorable childhood play experiences from Wellington, New Zealand?

Brian Sutton-Smith: Sure, I'll tell you some of my own ways of playing. We used to like to go past the grocery store where there were eggs outside on sale. We'd steal a few eggs and then walk about a hundred yards along the road where there was a big advert for the movies—flicks we called them. And we'd take the eggs, I'm afraid we were very sexist, and we'd try to hit the beautiful women's faces. We did that a few times. The last time was when the proprietor came running out and chased us. I was running up the street that was very shady, and I lay down in the gutter because there was no light there and it was dark. He came hammering past but didn't catch me. I stopped taking eggs from then on.

Another one was a wonderful game involving cow pots. Now a cow pot is a big round cow poop that dries on the surface but is still soft and sloppy underneath. And we had fights. You put your hand on top, scoop it out on the dry part, and then throw it at each other's faces. It was difficult as it would break and get on your clothes and your mother would go nuts. That was combined with horse dung grenades; use your imagination.

One of the other great childhood New Zealand amusements happened in the forest. After World War I a lot of people were out of work and so they were put to work planting pine trees. So, all round the hills were pine trees. When we started exploring the pine tree forests we found that these were the places where lovers went. If you went quietly through the trees you could find lovers doing their thing. We would be laughing and we couldn't stop ourselves. We'd take pinecones and throw them at the lovers. Several times we'd have great contact, and a pinecone would hit the back of the man doing his thing. Sometimes it would be ok, but sometimes the man would get up and chase us full of anger and we would run screaming down the tracks. They had tracks going through these pine trees and we would disappear lying behind a tree and hoping we didn't get caught. We didn't do this very often because it was too dangerous. I'm giving you the sort of flavor of New Zealand play.

Question: How did you first get involved in studying children's play?

Sutton-Smith: In New Zealand, I first started studying play because I was a teacher. We went through three years of training and in the last year you had a classroom of your own. What I found almost immediately was that there were no stories for children written in New Zealand and about New Zealand. They were all about British stuff, so I started to write. At that time I was a teacher in a Standard 3 School in Wellington, New Zealand—down in a big valley, down to the beach, raining all the time. I thought—okay I know all about this, and this is where the books that I wrote came from. 'Our Street' was my first book. It came by the end of the year; the others came later. I felt I was doing okay as the childhoods of the boys in my books were like my childhood. My stories reflected my own experiences. The kids loved them and I was doing well with them.

At that time they had journals for each age level with reading material in them, but never anything about New Zealand. A friend who was a teacher too was able to persuade the Education Department in Wellington, who were responsible for the journals to include my chapters and produce one each month, which for me was real glory. So they did, but there was an awful argument that came from the Headmasters Association about the slang that was being introduced to children via these stories, and the rather dubious morality of children stealing and things of that kind. In fact the issue got into the New Zealand parliament, and the conservatives (the National Party) argued that my stories should not be allowed, because they were full of slang, and gave a disgusting representation of the nature of New Zealand childhood. So they were banned, and I was sitting there thinking, what the hell is going on here? That's when I started to become famous. The Education Department stopped recommending the chapters, but of course they got published immediately. So they became famous in their own way, and because the books were banned they sold pretty well. In subsequent years, I wrote two more.

That interest in play became central to my life. All this happened at a time when I was completing a PhD. I'd done a Masters degree at Victoria University, Wellington, and then the PhD. With all the happenings in the school, I decided to make the PhD about games and play. During that time I travelled all over New Zealand and I found play everywhere. I didn't have enough money to travel so I used to travel with physical educationalists. They were very positive with me because I was into play, which was their life. I would go with them to different schools and ended up visiting about 30 of them. I slept much of the time in their car at night and it was frosty and wet. It was a hardship; I got quite sick at one time which was part of the art of doing this thing. I got all this data and put it together as I found it, and the kids' jokes are a part of it.

Question: Can you provide some background to the stories you wrote for the children in New Zealand?

Sutton-Smith: To my surprise the famous anthropologist Robert Fagen came up with a discussion of the three storybooks I had written about childhood in New Zealand. One was called 'Our Street,' one was called 'Smitty Does a Bunk' (that means runs away), and finally 'The Cobbers' (that's about fights between different groups and so on). What he said, I would never have had the gall to say myself, but it goes this way.

> In Sutton-Smith's Wellington play is earthy, physical, rough-edged, mischievous, subversive, competitive, occasionally cruel, not always fun, rarely lyrical and sometimes violent. Protagonists Brin and Smitty and their friends are real children, not idealised figments of romantic fantasy, they love to fight and squabble and slug it out. Their playful feistiness propels them into impromptu and organised sports, and through it all they manage to deepen their friendships, to grow and to mature and to hold on to some of their dreams. The boys build forts, have spitting contests, play pick-up versions of cricket and rugby, chant rude rhymes, visit the zoo and go to the movies where they yell, throw papers and apple cores and surreptitiously turn down seats so that their occupants fall flat when they try to sit down. Sutton-Smith recounts gritty wondrous truths of play as play close up and personal in the streets and backyards of depression era Wellington. His books, revolutionary children's literature in their day, remain nothing short of outstanding. And later in non-fiction works Sutton-Smith further illuminates the play histories of his native New Zealand.

What am I to think of this? It's quite exciting, and gives us an idea of how variable play can be in some situations. The difficulty of saying that this is how play is in New Zealand is that the girls are left out. In my book, 'Games for New Zealand Children,' I have a lot of female play.

The cover of the three kids books has a cartoon, and the characters are supposedly myself, my elder brother, who was always bashing me, and Horsey. Horsey's opinion was always his opinion; getting him to move was a pain in the arse. And there's Smitty, my brother who doesn't look especially brutal but he was a champion boxer who won his weight every year; so I thought I had to do that too. So I tried and I got beaten most of the time, but I did win one year. I was a welter-weight boxing champion for the year so that was kind of nice. I didn't go round punching people like my brother did, but nevertheless some imitation was afforded. Then there was Gormy, whose house it was. In New Zealand everything is on a hill, you have to find places to get the sun. Gormy's house had a front door porch, and we used to congregate there, trying to decide what we would do in the afternoon; trying to decide all those things that you have often heard me talk about. New Zealand is permanently windy and a little bit on the cool side and it rains all the time, so as a kid you run to school through the rain, and you have to run like hell.

Anyway, these are the four kids on the cover of the book, and they are try-ing to get it together and have some fun. They engage in the kind of play that people don't want to acknowledge some of the time, but it is pretty central to many street boys.

Question: Tell us about the importance of folklore studies in shaping your thinking about play.

Sutton-Smith: The really exciting thing that came my way was the work of Peter and Iona Opie. I met Peter in a bar in England, when I first went to England in the early 1950s. He and his wife had written books about the his-tory of literature for children. Apparently there was literature for kids to read way back for about a thousand years. He and I got talking, and I had just fin-ished my thesis, 900 pages of the games of New Zealand children, and he said "We don't have anything about play," so I talked him into doing play and the Opie's came out with the book *The Lore and Language of School Children*. It came out in 1959, and I came out with *The Games of New Zealand Children* at the same time, nowhere near the status of theirs of course. What excited me was the contents in their book that fit the six or seven categories that I've been talking about. Wow! The way they related the emotions to particular kinds of behavior derived from their information which had come from all over the British Isles, and mine was mainly from New Zealand. This was a validation that hit me over the head with a big bang.

So, I joined the folklore people. Actually I co-created the Children's Folklore Society because I found that I could learn more about gangs talking to folklore people, than to psychologists. Psychologists are trapped by their own need for an experiment. Good or bad as it may be, it doesn't take you to the world, whereas folklore is about traditions wherever they are.

Question: Can you share some examples of children's jokes that you collected?

Sutton-Smith: When I got a Fulbright scholarship to come to America, England, and elsewhere I travelled the world looking for play and for the arguments about play. So you go to Freud and Piaget of course, but I found some great folklorists who were really most helpful sending me stuff from all over the world. I'd written these books about kids play as they really were. That's what kids were like. People didn't want to think that they were like that, but they were—rough and ready.

When I got to Bowling Green State University as a Professor of Educational Psychology I had my own Masters students go out and find what jokes the

11 year olds in Ohio told. So here we go with some of the jokes from Ohio. If I was in trouble before . . . !

Mrs Jones, Nancy was run over by a steamroller. Oh just slide her under the door I'm taking a bath.

Mother can I go ice skating? No you cannot. Why not? The skates won't fit your crutches.

Mummy can I go up in the elevator? No your iron lung won't fit.

Mummy I don't want to go to China. Shut up and keep digging.

Mummy can we have a dog? Shut up and keep barking.

Mummy why is father running across the field? Shut up and reload the gun.

Hey mum why does dad always lose his head? Shut up and sharpen the axe.

Mummy why can't we get a garbage disposal? Shut up or I will flush it again.

Mummy it's dark down here. Shut up and put that pillow in place.

Mummy can I lick the bowl? Shut up and flush it like anyone else.

Mummy, mummy daddy is throwing up all over the bathroom. Why are you crying son? Because my sister is getting all the big pieces.

Oh mum I hate grandpa's guts. Shut up and eat what's put in front of you.

Mummy, mummy my little brother is on fire. Then hurry and get a marshmallow.

Mummy I want out of the closet. Shut up we don't want the fire to spread to the rest of the house. Mummy, mummy I'm tired of running in circles. Shut up or I will nail your other foot to the floor.

This was the beginning of my interest in humor. There are lots of them. Here are some more—verbal insults:

Your nose is like a faucet. Drip, drip, drip.

Your arse is grass and my fist is a lawnmower.

This is wonderful stuff, nobody else had ever, as far as I know made this available to the ordinary population.

Fatty, fatty, 2 by 4, can't get through the bathroom door. So he went all over the floor, licked it up and went some more.

Green, green gobs of juicy grimy gopher guts, mutilated monkey feet, chopped up a parakeet, eagles eyes, and a great big bowl of pus—and me without a spoon.

Do you know what is 4 feet long and hangs in the trees in Africa? Elephant snot.

Deformity jokes:

What is the name of a man with no arms and legs in the water? Bob.
What's the name of a man with no arms and legs coming in the mail? Bill.

It's this kind of material (and I have a lot more of it) that makes me think
if we are trying to understand play we'd better try and understand humour.
This is free floating stuff; these kids are making it up. We always say that
play gives you the freedom to make things up, to do what you like—free
play anyway. Now this seems to be happening in the humour, so what are the
parallels? I'm not trying to answer that just yet, but this is the sort of thing
I'm aiming for.

By the way there was a lot of nice African-American stuff too.

Listen my children and you shall hear of the midnight ride of diarrhoea.
Hasten Jason get the basin, oops plop, get the mop.
You're ma, you're pa, you're orphan Annie, you're greasy granny, you're
Frankenstein with a black behind, you're Cleopatra, you titty-snatcher.

This is more mature stuff as you can see:

A girl from Kansas City:
There's a girl from Kansas City. She's got meatballs for her titties. She's
got scrambled eggs between her legs. That's the girl from Kansas City.
I like coffee, I like tea, I like a coloured boy and he likes me.
Step back white boy cos you don't shine. I'll get a coloured boy to kick
your behind.

That's a brief group that indicates there is a lot of humor around, managed
by children. What I'm trying to do is to say how do I put it with those games
to identify common attitudes and so on.

Question: Can you share some examples of children's stories that you
collected?

Sutton-Smith: When I moved to Columbia University in New York I got my
MA students going on children's stories, and we collected hundreds of them.
They're all collected in a large book. I should tell you a few.

Here's a 2 year old:

The cat went on the cakie; the cat went in the car. The cookie was in my nose;
the cookie went on the fireman's hat. The fireman's hat went on the bucket, the

cookie went on the carousel, the cookie went on the puzzle; the cookie went on the doggie.

Not bad for two years of age. That's Alice.

The dog went on the popa; the popa went on the house; the house went on the pigeon.

Here's Beatrice, another 2 year old:

She makes pee on the floor. Then she goes with her mum to the Ferris wheel. Now she went home and saw her dada. And now the daddy went away. Now her grandpa is dead. Now she crept into her bed. Now she had a new baby. Her mother said no babies allowed. Now all the people were stuffy and had medicine. The end.

These are 2-year-old kids in pre-schools in New York City. I told my students to take the kids into the corridor and say, "Can you tell me your stories—I'd like to hear your stories" and the kids loved it. Anyway that's 2-year-olds and I have a lot of them like that, that are more perceptual—going from a to b to c to d.

These are from 7-year-olds:

Now there was a parked car boo boo. There was a dog do do. And you didn't like dog do do. Then there was a man named snowball, and he didn't like snow cha cha, choo choo, cha cha, choo choo. I named dog do do, Christopher say do do do. Then there was a boy named Torsor, oh do do. Then there was a Captain Bluper he had a hook and he was very bad and it hurt him. Then there was a blue pa pa pa, there was superman coming and you heard both him knees and then they were flying and they went right into the ocean and he got a bite from a shark and he didn't like when he got a bite from a shark, then Clark Clark to to, te ta.

This is the world upside down and it was published by the University of Pennsylvania Press. I was a double professor at the University of Pennsylvania. They made me a Professor of Folklore as well as a Professor of Developmental Psychology—and they courageously accepted all this stuff.
Felix:

A baby was walking down the street making trouble and when the baby saw a man passing her she said you suck your buggers two times yeh yeh. Then they went to a music studio and they heard "keep coming in a b c, a b c, 1 2 3" And then the baby said "I can do the whole alphabet abcdefg . . . tuvwxyz, that's how." Then the baby said I spit at you. And then she spitted in the air.

Then the baby said abc my bugger. Then the baby said I think I'm so smart just because I have one more tooth out. Then the baby said I am superman you can't hurt superman.

This goes on for a couple of pages so if you forgive me we can stop.
Here's an 8-year-old: The Gerbil:

Once upon a time there was a gerbil and it liked to play. He always sticks his nose out of the cage and I tickle it. Sometimes he bites me but I don't care because it doesn't hurt that much. He has a nice bottle that he sleeps in that's full of colours that shredded cardboard. He always tries to climb up the water bottle I love him. The end.

This is very relevant to the way we should go. This is a 9-year-old:

It's about a murderer and use swords, daggers, knives, spears, nun chucks, and different types of stars. He pokes people's eyes out with files and daggers. He pokes people's eyes out with chick blocks. He beats people up in their stomach with nun chucks with three sticks.

Pretty good when you're 9 years.
Olive 10 years:

Henry Tick. Chapter One.

A few years ago Henry Tick lived in a hippy's hair but he got a crew cut so Henry had to move. He went to the dog pound but it was closed. He went to the pet shop but it was closed too. He finally found a nice basset hound so he moved in. He got a good job in the circus jumping 2 inches in the air into a glass of water. One day he jumped but there was no water. He was rushed to the hospital. They put 12 stitches into his leg. Well he never went there again. The end.

You're getting quite mature stuff here. It's wild, isn't it? I'm glad I'm reading it to you. I hadn't realized how wild it is. This is fantasy, and I think all of this is making pretend into a function a bit like any other function. I think we tend to assume pretend is functional in more rational kinds of ways, and that's a big mistake.

Question: What were you trying to find out when you began working on *The Ambiguity of Play*?

Sutton-Smith: When I began to talk seriously about play I collected every kind of play I could, and I found play that was of different kinds. There is solitary play, mind play, playful behaviours, informal social play, various audiences' play, performance play, celebrations and festivals, contests, games and sports, risky or deep play—in fact I found 308 different types of play. So what is one going do with that? There is just an incredible amount of it and that's what I am going to struggle with today.

In 1997 I published a book called 'The Ambiguity of Play' trying to come to grips with the question 'what the heck is play'? How can it be all these 308 phenomena? And I came up with what I call the rhetorics of play, which are basically the major forms that people argue in favour of. In the Ambiguity book I included plays about progress, plays that are about fate, plays that are about power, plays that are about identity, plays that are about the imaginary, plays that are about self, and plays that are about frivolity. I made these the seven major ways that play is. What good was that? Well, you discover when you look at all these that there are modern forms and there are ancient forms.

Modern forms are the ones where people talk about the psychological development that is going on in the play form whereas in a more historical and literary stance there are those that seem to be talking about play as types of imagination. Back in Kant's time there was a great change in science that had been orientated towards perceptions until that point. Instead, he suggested that imagination was always involved; hypotheses that were created were the result of imagination, which could be positive or negative. So the fifth rhetoric is about play that is imagination. The sixth rhetoric is really about the self—a modern preoccupation with ontology. This play is about the subjectivity of the agent. That's a couple of the modern ones.

Then we get the ancient ones, which have been around much longer. The main one is all about contests, and the winners and losers. That's the big one in most cases, but also there are play forms that are about membership, and that's what you get in festivals and that sort of stuff. Then there is another one about risk; that's about gambling, and jumping off mountains and parachutes and so on. And finally there is nonsense and that's for the tricksters.

So, I had myself seven rhetorics three modern and four ancient but where did that get me? Well I had a real breakthrough when Antonio Damasio, a neurologist, said there are several types of emotion—and I've got seven rhetorics of play. Now I've got to make that work, so I began to look at his emotions. Damasio said there are two types—primary and secondary. The primary emotions are shock, anger, fear, disgust, sadness and joy. And then there are the secondary emotions, which are empathy, pride, envy, embarrassment, guilt, and shame.

And then we get people like the famous neurologist Panksepp, who was at Bowling Green State University. I knew this guy was doing something interesting, but I had no idea it was going to be as good as it was. He was able to locate the primary emotions in the amygdala area, in the centre of the brain, and the regulative emotions at the front of the brain, the conceptual part of the brain. The primary emotions are called reptile emotions, universal emotions, survival emotions, amygdala dominant emotions, first-year-of-life emotions, negative emotions, involuntary emotions, reflexive emotions, and destructive emotions. Now we're starting to get complicated, but these things can all be fitted to the primary emotions. The secondary emotions are sometimes called mammal emotions, cultural emotions, familial emotions, neo-cortical and dominant emotions, seventy-year onward emotions, positive emotions, voluntary emotions, social emotions, and compassionate emotions.

So what am I going to do now? I find that the rhetorics sort of match these primary and secondary emotions. How do I match Damasio's emotions with the phenomenon of play? For example, anger: what sort of a play fits that? Children's insults, gangs, jeers, torments, mean play, spoilsports, cheats, bullies, school rivalries, paints, jewels, food fights, riddles, jokes, tic-tac-toe, checkers, chess, video games, rough and tumble, play fighting of all kinds; also adult's games of physical contest such as football, wrestling, boxing, ice hockey, basketball, baseball and symbolic contests such as board chess, checkers, video and computer games. They are all governed consciously or otherwise by anger, by the design of attack, to defeat, to win. So that's the contest phenomenon. Now I can do the same sort of thing with fear, disgust, sadness, and joy. It gets assimilated into the world of play.

What do I do then? Well, I went around trying to match some of the other things. The world was suffering from all kinds of people's other ideas. Take Kant who talks about player's imagination; Schiller who talks about aesthetics; Groos who talks about orderly work; Spencer who talks about lower faculties; Freud who talks about instinctive or regressive expressions; Ericsson who talks about true or pseudo play; Winnicott who talks about instinctive or scaffolded play; Piaget who talks about cognition distortion or assimilation; and so on and so on. There are all these other forms of looking at play; they're all available. So my job is to hang in and make it go the way I suggested it could go.

Question: How has your thinking evolved since publishing *The Ambiguity of Play*?

Sutton-Smith: My general mental attitude now is that we won't be able to understand play until we at least understand play and humour, and play and narrative. I'm making these statements because throughout my career I have collected lots of evidence. There may be other big bags of variables, but these three are all the sort of things that children do. At the very least I'm trying to find similarities across what are otherwise thought to be very different disciplines. What I will try to communicate to you is an answer to what play is really about. I think we can only really understand it if we take play and humour and stories (which are three things I've spent a lot of time on), and find mutual frameworks across them. It's only when we do so, that we really understand what we are doing.

I have worked up a pending book called '*Play as Emotional Survival.*' I will argue in that book that if we want to think about play we have to think about it as more of a mythology. Now a mythology has all sorts of movements and all sorts of angles and there's usually a spiritual aspect. I began to play with that idea and it gradually came to me that if I want to understand play I also need to understand stories and narrative. Children do that too; they make up stories as part of their play; but even more important they make up jokes and humour. So if I could find the pattern that goes with play as myriadly described, and humour which is of all kinds, and the narrative which is sto-ries, then we might have a grasp of this mythology, whatever it is, and the way the emotions are shared across it.

I feel the model for these stories and jokes is dreams. We keep on finding models for the other things that children do from other human actions. I've got to work this out a bit more clearly of course. The kids start from their dreams; they start from the way the mind can do anything, anything they've ever thought. If they told their mothers about some of the stuff they thought they would get it in the neck. We've not paid enough attention to night dreams. If you want to know what the source of these stories and jokes is, it might just be the night dreams.

The play forms are the light of day. They are more conditioned; they are more our language. We like studying them because we can make them more rational, but is it really so rational? Take a look at people at soccer matches. If you look at the stands, there's thousands of people yelling and screaming. The game allows them to be angry. I remember a student I had once who was going to basketball. He said "It's the only time I get to scream." We don't in ourselves recognise that there are many daytime things that are as bad as the bad dream- time. It's kind of the basic nastiness the basic earthiness is to be found in the dream-like world. The mind can do any damn thing it likes in a dream, and the earliest statements that imitate this are found in children's play.

Not all children's play is nasty; it gets educated and gets trained. When I was a teacher you had to go around the playground because some play was just nasty as hell. Kids who were playing marbles had a hell of a hard job saving them. In the game of scragging one kid is in the middle and everybody else comes charging through the middle and he's got to catch one and bang him three times. Then you were in the middle and you were allowed to bash them in the back, bang, bang, bang. We had a playground field that was not as big as a football field but it was a long run and gradually the group in the middle got bigger and bigger as you got caught. Finally no kids could get through and they got scragged. Some kids weren't allowed to play because their shirts got ripped. But most of us wanted to be rugby players, so scragging was a good game.

This is near to primitivism, and I would give dreams the root credit for the fact that the mind can do any damn thing, and you are taught not to have those sorts of dreams. My wife would wake up screaming in the middle of the night. She would completely lose it, but that was all part of the foundry of the dream life. I learned that if I leaned over and took hold of her arm, she would stop. Just a touch in the night on the arm or leg and the devil disappears you know.

Jokes are like that too. You get more freedom from a joke and you can go to hell in one way or another. So when nice people try to understand children playing the forces of nature are against what they want to do. I'm not saying we should give way to all this sort of stuff, but we might allow a certain amount of wildness. I think that what I'm advocating here is that pretend play is not just make-believe in a sweet way. It's much more important than we realise. We need to investigate pretend play more than we have done—the madness of pretence, not just the rationality of pretence.

Now this is an advocacy that would not be very popular. I suppose that civilisation says we should fight against all that kind of thing, but maybe we shouldn't. For that sort of thing, particularly in play terms, we have to make a very large allowance. I haven't quite got it stated correctly yet. There has to be limits I realise, but we try to make these things rational somehow, and that doesn't quite do them justice. There are places where the madness of the human mind is expressed—take a look at those madmen in those audiences. People go on like crazy.

I should write a novel actually, nobody's going to believe this anyway. They're not going to know what to do with it except have a lot of fun I hope.

Chapter 9

Brian Does a Prank

Jay Mechling

[Author's Note: This story is inspired by Brian Sutton-Smith's novel, *Smitty Does a Bunk* (1961), the second of three novels he wrote based on his experience playing as a child in the 1930s in a suburb of Wellington, New Zealand. The first was *Our Street* in 1950 and the third was *The Cobbers* in 1976. Sutton-Smith also published an autobiographical essay on his experience playing as a child and the role of those experiences in his theorizing about play, but these three novels stand alone as examples of a little-used genre of writing, autoethnography, that has great value in reflecting on the personal *experience* of childhood play. It should be noted that Brian faced displeasure from the school authorities and other adults in his depiction of how real boys play and talk, instead of some idealized fantasy of innocent New Zealand boyhood. My story is very much in the spirit of Brian.]

"So, what's the plan?" asked Tommy.

"You guys go to my tent as quietly as you can. Tell Jayden I'll be there soon with Robby. The plan is like the one when we initiated you, Russ. I tell a scary story, we send Robby alone into the woods, Jayden hides along the path, scares the Hershey squirts out of Robby, who then runs back to us."

"Okay," said Tommy, as he squirmed out of his sleeping bag and grabbed his pants—as did Russ. Brian turned and crawled back out into the moonshine, then headed for Robby's tent. He needed to wake up Robby quietly because Robby's tentmate, Tyler, belonged to a different patrol and Brian did not want Tyler to know about the hazing and initiation he had planned for Robby. The Scoutmaster made it clear to the boys he did not tolerate hazing of any sort. That did not deter Brian.

He found Robby's tent and kneeled at the front door, quietly unzipped the flaps and stuck the top half of his body on all fours into the tent. In the dark he saw two sleeping bags, each stuffed with a twelve-year-old boy. But which sleeping bag held Robby, he wondered.

"Well," thought Brian, "it's a 50–50 chance," and he reached out his hand to touch the feet of one of the boys through the foot of his sleeping bag, and the boy stirred.

"Robby?" whispered Brian.

"Yeah, is that you Brian?" Brian was relieved he had not awakened Tyler, who was lightly snoring, in training for his snoring as an adult leader, thought Brian.

"What's wrong?" whispered Robby, surprised to be awakened late at night.

"Get dressed and follow me. Don't wake up Tyler. Tonight is your initiation into the patrol."

"Okay," whispered Robby, clearly excited. Brian withdrew and stood by the door flaps until Robby emerged. Without a word, Brian turned and strode back to the tent he and Jayden shared. Robby followed a few steps behind, like an obedient puppy. Robby admired Brian and wanted to be like him and be liked by him. Once they got to the tent, Brian held open one of the flaps and gestured to Robby to enter the tent. Brian followed and closed the flap behind him.

Jayden, Tommy, and Russ were already sitting cross-legged along the walls of the tent. The small lantern sat in the center of their circle on the floor of the tent, casting the boys' shadows onto the tent walls, a perfect background for a scary story. The tent was designed for two boys to sleep in, so with five boys it was a bit crowded, but the boys did not mind touching knees in their circle and their bodies actually warmed up the tent a bit. They sat silent for about a minute.

"So," began Brian, speaking softly, "we of the Bear patrol are assembled here to initiate Robby into the patrol." The boys all looked at Robby, who smiled.

"This is serious," Brian scolded Robby, who quickly wiped the grin off his face and tried to look solemn.

"Initiating new members into the patrol is a long tradition in the troop," continued Brian. "You will have to pass a test, Robby, to prove yourself worthy of the brotherhood of the Bear patrol." The boys nodded solemnly in agreement.

"First, though, I want to tell you a story, Robby. It's part of the test of your courage and loyalty to the brothers. You have to trust us."

Robby muttered "I do."

"That's good, Robby, so here is the story. You know Sapp's Cabin, that run-down remains of a cabin out on Sapp's meadow where we hiked to the large lake?"

"Yeah," said Robby, wide-eyed.

"Well, Robby, there is a story about that cabin. Jeremiah Sapp was a gold prospector who built that cabin years ago. He mined for gold and he had a few sheep up there on the meadow. Nobody ever found his gold mine, and one year he just disappeared. The sheep wandered away and the cabin just got old and collapsed finally from the mountain weather."

Robby was rapt, as were the other boys, who had heard the story before but were always swept up with Brian's skill at telling stories. They leaned in, so as not to miss any part of Brian's whispered story.

"Actually, Sapp did not live alone in that cabin. He had a son with him, folks say, but the mother left them both. She hated the wilderness and went back to her family in San Francisco, so they say. So, it was just Jeremiah Sapp and his son, Jacob, living in that cabin."

Brian paused, letting Robby think that was all there was to his story. But there was more.

"One night Jacob went outside in the dark to gather some firewood for their stove. He never came home. Jeremiah was frantic. He went to the edge of the meadow, where the forest began, to look for Jacob and on the ground was the axe Jacob had carried with him for chopping the firewood. Jeremiah picked up the axe and saw blood on the blade."

At the word "blood" a few of the boys, even those who had heard the story before, visibly shuddered. Robby's widening eyes showed Brian his story was having the effect he intended.

"People say that Jeremiah never found Jacob, that Jeremiah never knew if the blood on the axe blade was human blood or bear blood. Jeremiah searched the forest for Jacob, holding the axe in case a bear attacked, but he never found Jacob. People say Jeremiah went crazy from the grief and that on nights with full a moon like tonight he roams the forest looking for Jacob, carrying the bloody axe and calling out his name. Jaaaaaaacob. Jaaaaaaaacob. Jaaaaaaaaaaacob. Like that."

The boys were quiet, though Jayden was smirking a little.

After a dramatic pause, Brian broke the spell the story cast. "And now for the initiation. Follow me, boys." One-by-one they crawled out of the tent and stood in the moonlight. Brian started talking, which distracted the boys from observing that Jayden quietly slipped away from the group and headed for the forest.

"So here is what is going to happen, Robby," explained Brian. "We want you to display the courage we expect in a member of the Bear Patrol. You know the place we call Inspiration Point? It's about three hundred yards in that direction," said Brian, as he pointed into the forest. "You are going to walk from here, alone, to Inspiration Point, pick up a flag we left there stuck in the sand, and bring us back that Bear patrol flag. Understand?"

Robby nodded, he understood.

"Good. Get the flag, come back to us, and you will have shown us the courage and trust we expect in a brother in the Bear patrol."

With that, Brian took Robby by the shoulders, turned him around to face in the right direction, and gave him a gentle push to start walking. They watched Robby walk cautiously to the boundary of the camp, watched him nervously look over his shoulder at the other boys, and then watched him walk into the forest, hearing the crunch and crack of twigs and leaves grow fainter as he moved farther away from them, step-by-step, until they could no longer hear him.

"That story gets me every time," said Russ. "Gives me goosebumps." He noticed that Jayden was not with them. "Ah, I guess Jayden is out there already to moan 'Jaaaaacob, Jaaaaacob.'"

"Yeah," said Brian. Just like Tad did when he initiated you. You came back to us white as a ghost."

"Nah, I knew it was a prank all the time."

"Sure you did," needled Tommy. "So why did you have to wash out your underwear after you got back?"

"Very funny," said Russ. "No kidding. I really did know it was a prank."

"Well, you sure gave a good imitation of a kid who saw a ghost."

"Why do we do this anyway?" asked Tommy. "Scoutmaster Pete always says, 'no hazing.' We call this an initiation but really it's hazing, isn't it? He yelled at me the other day for doing the Atomic Sit-ups prank with a new kid. He got really mad at me and said that was hazing and he won't tolerate hazing. I thought it was just a prank. Nobody was hurt."

Brian thought for a moment. "Yeah, I guess our initiations are hazing, but I think that's pretty common in fraternities and sports teams in college, and probably in other Boy Scout troops. And it's always in secret. My brother is in a frat at the university, and he told me about the ways they haze pledges, make them get naked and do stuff. Humiliating stuff. I asked my brother how he could do that, and he told me, 'so you can show your frat brothers you can take it like a man, take pain and humiliation to prove you want to belong to the frat.' That's what he said. I guess that's why we do what we do to bring new kids into the Bear patrol."

Tommy frowned. "I dunno, it seems kinda mean to me."

"But you did it," said Brian. "You could have refused and joined another patrol or even left the troop, but you didn't. You stuck with it, and we welcomed you into the patrol."

Tommy sighed. "I did not want to chicken out, have the guys think I am a pussy. I would have felt terrible walking away. I think the fear was easier to take than the shame." Tommy looked like he was about to cry, remembering those feelings.

Brian stepped up to Tommy and gave him a hug. "You made the right choice, Tommy. We love you. You can always count on us."

Russ gazed up at the sky and said "Man, it's cold tonight. I hope Robby runs back soon so we can warm up in our tents again. It's colder than a witch's tit out here."

"Do you have to talk that way, Russ?"

"Uh, yeah I do, Brian. Besides," continued Russ," one of the most important things a kid learns at Scout camp is how to curse and say bad words. Like 'fuck' - fuckin this and fuckin that."

"Jayden told me that after his first year at camp," agreed Brian, "when he got home, he slipped one night at the dinner table and asked his sister to 'please pass the fucking butter.' His mother almost fell off her chair, but his dad just smiled. Jayden was so used to the way we talk at camp."

"That's the difference between moms and dads," said Tommy. "Moms and sisters think we're gross. Dads and brothers think we're just normal boys."

Russ looked off to the edge of the forest. "Shouldn't Robby have come running back to camp by now?"

Brian looked at the edge of the forest where Robby had gone into the trees. "Yeah, it is taking a long time. Jayden should have scared him by now."

Suddenly Jayden emerged from the dark edge of the forest into the moonlit campsite and walked up to the boys, carrying the axe.

"Robby never showed up," said Jayden. "I waited and waited. When I thought I waited long enough I started walking back here and along the way something strange happened."

"Strange?" asked Brian.

"Yeah, I was sure I heard a voice over to my right and I am pretty sure I heard the voice moan Jaaaaacob. Jaaaacob. Freaked me out."

"Very funny, Jayden, but where is Robby?"

"I swear I never saw him."

"Scout's honor?" asked Brian, beginning to panic.

"Scout's honor. I never saw Robby and I swear I heard someone calling out Jacob's name."

The color left Brian's face. "Oh no."

Chapter 10

Brian Sutton-Smith and Anything Goes

"A carnevale ogni scherzo vale"

Helen Schwartzman

During carnival in Italy there is an expression used frequently, *"A carnevale ogni scherzo vale,"* which means that during carnival, *anything goes*, or all tricks count. You can play whatever kind of fun, practical joke or trick on someone and they must accept it as "carnival fun." I don't know if Brian was familiar with this tradition but he certainly practiced the sentiment in his life and research. When I think about Brian what I remember most was his ability to think about play with an "anything goes" attitude. What I mean by this is that Brian eagerly embraced multiple perspectives on play and the history of his scholarship illustrates how wide-ranging his research was and also how he embraced multiple theoretical perspectives to develop his understanding of play. This approach is illustrated in his early studies that examined the effects of European games on Māori children games in New Zealand and his later concern with the dramatic, improvisational, reversible and transgressive characteristics of children's play. Brian's views were expansive and always evolving and this is probably most evident in his book entitled *The Ambiguity of Play* (2001) where he lays out his enormously flexible orientation to the study of play; and, it really is an "anything goes" approach.

I was fortunate to be involved in the formation and early years of the one organization that focused specific attention on the study of play by anthropologists (and other researchers as well). The organization was called The Association for the Anthropological Study of Play (TAASP, a mouthful to say) and it was founded in 1976 and over the next 15/20 years many of the major scholars, whose research examined both the how and the why of play in

95

human and non-human animals, participated in the organization's activities, giving papers and organizing sessions at annual meetings as well as serving as featured speakers at these events. Brian was an important guiding force for this organization but we were fortunate to have virtually all of the researchers who were thinking creatively about play at this time as participants in TAASP programs. The list would include: Edward Bruner, Victor Turner, Brian Sutton-Smith, Michael Salter, Mihalyi Csikszmenthalyi, Gregory Bateson, John M. Roberts, Helen B. Schwartzman, Philip Stevens, David Lancy, Frank E. Manning, Cindy Dell Clark and many, many others. To get a sense of what I would say is the "Brianesque" (aka anything goes) approach to play that was characteristic of these meetings a review of the contents of several of the early publications of TAASP proceedings illustrates the expansive **A** ("Anti-School Parodies as Speech Play and Social Protest" by Marilyn Jorgenson, 1983) to **Z** ("Playing a Kingdom: A Hausa Meta-Society in the Walled City of Zaria, Nigeria" by Harold Olofson, 1977) approach characteristic of these meetings.

Brian was an amazing person, and I am so appreciative of the support that he gave to my work on play. I think that what was most exceptional about Brian was his amazing ability to speak about play playfully. This is something that very few people can do, at least in my experience. I guess another way of saying this is that Brian was the epitome of meta when it came to play. Anyone who was lucky enough to hear him speak at a meeting will know exactly what I mean with this description. One of my favorite memories, that illustrates this ability of Brian to embody play in his research presentation-performances, was hearing him retell some of the stories created by the children who participated in the research reported in *The Folkstories of Children* (1981, University of Pennsylvania Press, collaborators: Daniel M. Abrams, Gilbert J. Botvin, M'Lou Caring, Daniel P. Gildesgame, Daniel H. Mahony, Thomas R. Stevens). My very favorite story, that appears in this book, is one that Brian often told whenever he spoke about this project. The story was originally told by Ingbert and it literally embodies the essence of a story and, in an important sense, the essence of Brian and his playful "anything goes" approach to play.

> *Once upon a time the once upon a time ate the once upon a time*
> *which ate the once upon a time*
> *and then the once upon a time which ate the once upon a time*
> *ate the princess once upon a time with the king.*
> *and then the once upon a times died*
> *then the end ate the end*
> *the end died*
> *the end died*
> *then the end died*

> *then the end died*
> *then the end died*
> *then the end died*
> *and then the end the end the end died*
> *the end with a the end*
> *the end*
> *the end*
> Ingbert, age 5 (Sutton-Smith, et al., 1981:114)

Once upon a time there was a trickster who played with play and his name was Brian Sutton-Smith. As a trickster he challenged and inverted our assumptions about play and he teased and championed the unruly and reversible qualities of this activity. I was lucky to know him and all play researchers, now and in the future, will continue to benefit from his "anything goes" approach to the topic of play.

"A carnevale ogni scherzo vale"

REFERENCES

Jorgenson, Marilyn. 1983. "Anti-School Parodies as Speech Play and Social Protest." In *The World of Play*, Frank E. Manning, ed. West Point, NY: Leisure Press. Proceedings of the Seventh Annual Meeting of The Association for the Anthropological Study of Play, pp. 91–102.

Olofson, Harold. 1977. "Playing a Kingdom: A Hausa Meta-Society in the Walled City of Zaria, Nigeria." In *The Study of Play: Problems and Prospects*, David F. Lancy and B. Allan Tindall, eds. West Point, NY: Leisure Press. Proceedings of the First Annual Meeting of The Association for the Anthropological Study of Play, pp. 167–175.

Sutton-Smith, Brian. 1981. *The Folkstories of Children* (with Daniel M. Abrams, Gilbert J. Botvin, M'Lou Caring, Daniel P. Gildesgame, Daniel H. Mahony, Thomas R. Stevens), Philadelphia, PA: University of Pennsylvania Press.

Sutton-Smith, Brian. 2001. *The Ambiguity of Play*. Cambridge, MA: Harvard University Press.

Chapter 11

Metaphorical Explorations of Play and Playwork

Fraser Brown

When I first met Brian Sutton-Smith he had been invited to be the keynote speaker at a playwork conference in the UK. I had been 'volunteered' to chaperone his UK visit and awaited his arrival at Manchester airport with some trepidation. All I knew of him was what I had read in his books. Consequently, I expected to meet a double-barrelled academic intellectual. Instead, I was confronted with one of the most playful people I had ever met. Within half an hour of the car journey to my home, we had become firm friends. This had to do with our common sense of humour, our love of sport, our shared belief in the strength of storytelling as a medium of explanation, and above all our interest in play as a powerful force in both individual and species development.

Despite this instant connection and the fact that he was due to speak at a playwork conference, Brian expressed his disquiet at the concept of playwork, which at the time he mistakenly equated with play 'leadership.' He had expected his playwork audience to challenge a lot of his ideas. Instead, they gave him a birthday party and baked him a cake. In fact, to his great surprise and enjoyment, many in the audience made it clear that they regarded him as a latter-day guru for their work.

Of course, the idea of 'leading' a child's play is anathema to the playwork profession. At its most basic level, the role of a playworker is to provide an environment within which children are free to play as they wish—something that is quite rare in many modern cultures, where children's freedom is routinely restricted because they tend to be regarded as either dangerous monsters or little angels in need of protection. The playwork approach[1] has many unique characteristics, summed up as follows:

THE UNIQUE ELEMENTS OF PLAYWORK

- A conceptualisation of the child that actively resists dominant and sub-ordinating narratives and practices.
- A belief that while playing, the 'being' child is far more important than the 'becoming' child.
- An adherence to the principle that the vital outcomes of playing are derived by children in inverse proportion to the degree of adult involvement in the process.
- A non-judgemental acceptance of the children as they really are, running hand in hand with an attitude, when relating to the children, of 'unconditional positive regard.'
- An approach to practice that involves a willingness to relinquish adult power, suspend any preconceptions, and work to the children's agenda.
- The provision of environments that are characterised by flexibility, so that the children are able to create (and possibly destroy and recreate) their own play environments according to their own needs.
- A general acceptance that risky play can be beneficial, and that intervention is not necessary unless a safety or safeguarding issue arises.
- A continuous commitment to deep personal reflection that manages the internal relationship between their present and former child-self, and the effects of that relationship on their current practice. (Brown, Long & Wragg 2018, p.717)

None of this requires the playworker to 'lead' the children during their play—quite the opposite. Indeed, there is no other profession which is quite so prepared to let the children 'get on with it.' In the distant past, when I was managing an adventure playground, we just had one rule: 'you can do whatever you want, so long as you don't stop another child enjoying themselves.'

Given that sort of play-full environment, play can be quite magical. So, it is not surprising that when we talk to adults about their most powerful childhood memory, the thing they generally get most energised about is a time when they were playing—most especially a time when they were free from adult control, free to roam, to explore, to experiment, to make their own friendships, to solve their own problems, etc.

Brian's classic text, *The Ambiguity of Play* (1997) sets out better than most the many ways in which children benefit <u>while</u> they are playing. I feel the word 'while' is significant here. We so often hear the statement that 'children learn and develop through their play,' but the word 'through' suggests the purpose of play is to help children achieve adulthood. I favour the statement that children learn and develop 'while' they are playing, because this lays the emphasis much more on the here and now.

Among the many things I discussed with Brian was the way in which children develop life skills while they are playing. Most of these skills cannot be taught (e.g., a theory of mind, sympathy, empathy, mimesis, etc.). Parents and teachers may encourage children to be aware of the feelings of other children, but these life skills are largely learned through active engagement with the world around us, and most especially in the child's social world. For example:

- During social play, children come to understand that they sometimes experience something in an entirely different way from the way in which their friends experience the same event (this strengthens the development of a 'theory of mind').
- Children learn to show sympathy when their friends experience pain—if not, then they may find themselves short of playmates in the future.
- If they misinterpret what their friends are doing when they engage in mimesis by using their body to represent a lion or an aeroplane, then their friends will feel uncomfortable, and future play opportunities may be limited.

At the heart of many of these life skills is the fact that babies come into the world with an understanding of the concept of rhythm, developed inside the mother's womb. Trevarthen (2005) suggests infants use that understanding to build a range of life skills during their play. If a playworker is well attuned to these life skills, then they may be able to create a suitable social and emotional environment for children's individual needs. Rhythm, sympathy, empathy, mimesis, affective attunement—all of these are present in the following story. In the case of Liliana, by using the simple device of a rhythmical song to help her feel secure, I was able to form a relationship very quickly.[2]

LILIANA—AUTHOR'S REFLECTION

In the summer of 2005, I was training a group of Romanian playworkers who were working in a paediatric hospital with a group of abandoned children. On my final day I came upon a very agitated 4-year-old girl who had been left in a ward totally alone. She stood at the bars of her cot rocking back and forth, making strange hooting noises. Every so often she walked rapidly round the cot, before settling back into her rocking.

Her doctors said she was "blind and mentally retarded." I felt uncomfortable with this diagnosis, as she was clearly aware of my presence, and appeared to be reacting to my movements (albeit not in a very positive fashion). There was obviously something wrong with her eyesight, but a quick experiment with moving lights showed she had some level of residual vision—seeing shadows, at the very least. An added complication was her fear of men's voices. This was confirmed when I called her name, "Liliana." Straight away she retreated to the back of the cot.

The playworkers were wondering how they could work with her. How could they get beyond the obstacle of her poor sight?

I started singing to Liliana quietly: "Twinkle, Twinkle, Little Star." She calmed down immediately, moving her head to locate the sound. At the end of the song, she made a noise in the back of her throat, which I interpreted as a request to sing again—a kind of play cue. I did this three times, and each time she moved closer to the sound.

Then, I started to clap gently in time to the rhythm of the song. When I stopped, she reached for my hands and put them together—another cue for me to sing. I repeated the song three more times, and each time she gave the same cue. On the last occasion she not only took my hands, but also started clapping them together in time to the song. Finally, she picked up the rhythm of the song in her own hand movements and clapped in time to my singing.

This whole sequence took no more than five minutes. In that short space of time, I was able to show the Romanian playworkers how to start making a relationship with Liliana by using rhythm and music.

Later that afternoon I went back into her ward, to find her rocking and hooting again. I called her name, "Liliana." She came across the cot and felt for my hands. Clasping them together in hers, she started to clap our hands together in a rhythm that I recognized - "Twinkle, Twinkle, Little Star." This was truly a magic moment

* * *

During play, Pedersen (2023, p.77) suggests, "we can instantly become collective choreographers in interweaving patterns of multiple forms of movement and rhythm." Perhaps that was what happened with this child. Liliana had been given negative labels by the medical profession because of her visual problems and attendant strange behaviour, but it was important not to be misled by her disability. She was just as able as any other child to learn and develop while she played. Adopting an open-minded, non-prejudicial, non-judgmental approach, which Fisher (2008) calls 'negative capability,' is an essential element of playwork. It makes it easy for the playworker to interpret the children's play cues accurately. In the case of Liliana, it was important to absorb her little noises, and her clasping of my hands, and understand that those cues were an invitation to repeat the song. My being able to interpret and respond appropriately to Liliana's play cues carried a strong message for her: i.e., this is someone who respects me; this is someone to be trusted. The fact that many hours later we were able to pick up the playful activity where we had left it demonstrates the strength of the playful connection.

That leads me on to another example of the power of playful connections—namely my concept of the 'therapist toddler.' This is the idea that enabling developmentally damaged children to engage in play with a toddler who is engaged in age-appropriate play might enable the older children to recover. I explore this here because Brian was especially taken with the concept when we discussed our work in Romania in the early part of this Century. Also, I recently discovered I have never written about the concept, despite having talked about it in detail in dozens of presentations in the last twenty years (e.g., 2018 Longfellow Lecture). The concept is rooted in two main sources:

- Suomi & Harlow (1971) reflecting on their work with infant monkeys reared in complete isolation. Here they discuss the 'therapist monkey' concept.
- Brown & Webb (2005) reflecting on our work with abandoned and neglected children in a Romanian paediatric hospital. This includes substantial exploration of the parallels between our work with children and the experiments of Suomi & Harlow with infant monkeys.

In the mid-20th Century, the psychologist Harry Harlow conducted a series of experiments which involved removing baby monkeys from their mothers at birth and rearing them in complete isolation. Harlow's often brutal research[3] showed the importance of caregiving and play to the development of social skills and cognition in his infant monkeys. He suggested the same would be true of all primates, including human children. Indeed, there are numerous parallels with our work in Romania, but these have been covered in detail in our article *Children Without Play* (mentioned above) and elsewhere. It is not my intention to cover that ground in this chapter. Suffice it to say, Harlow showed that isolation had a severely damaging impact on an infant monkey's chances of maturing into a stable functioning adult. Harlow and his collaborators suggested that play, or the absence of play, was a critical factor in this process. A little play in the developing years and the ill-effects of isolation appeared to be negated. The final sentence of their 1971 article is poignant and particularly relevant to our work in Romania:

> 'Then pity the monkeys who are not permitted to play, and pray that all children will always be allowed to play.' (Suomi and Harlow 1971: 495)

One aspect of Harlow's experiments that has received little attention is his concept of the 'therapist monkey.' Over many years, Harlow's work had produced dozens of highly damaged juvenile monkeys. He tried several methods to help them recover. The most successful was when he introduced a normally developing baby monkey into the cage of one of his damaged juveniles. The impact on the juvenile was substantial. It was as if the presence of a baby monkey engaged in age-related play enabled the damaged monkey to go back to the beginning and start again.

The parallels with our work with the Romanian children are striking. Those children had been abandoned at birth, and spent their lives largely ignored in a hospital ward. The impact was catastrophic. It was difficult to verify their ages, but some were definitely as old as ten or twelve. They had all been tied in their cots for years, isolated from any social contact, and generally neglected. By default, their life experience had been similar to that of Harlow's monkeys.

However, we were able to work with them in a playroom set aside for us by the new Director of the paediatric hospital. During a period when nothing changed in their lives, other than their introduction to the therapeutic playwork project, the children themselves changed dramatically. Their social interaction became more complex; physical activity showed a distinct move from gross to fine motor skills; the children's understanding of the world around them was improved; and they began to play in highly creative ways. They no longer sat rocking, staring vacantly into space. Instead, they had become fully engaged active human beings. All this happened in around 9 months—thus challenging the suggested timeframes of the various 'ages and stages' theories of child development.

Although we engaged in some highly focused one-to-one work with the children (as in the earlier example of Liliana), it is my contention that the primary reason for the children's rapid developmental recovery was the fact they were able to play with each other in an environment that was rich in 'fun, freedom, and flexibility' (Brown 2014) which is at the heart of the playwork approach.

This process was given greater impact than might otherwise have been the case by the presence of a normally developing toddler in the group. There was nothing contrived or unethical about this. In fact, I only appreciated his influence after the event. Pure chance meant that as we started the playwork project, this one-year-old child had recently been abandoned and had only just started being tied into his cot. As far as we could tell, his development thus far had not been seriously damaged. So, here was our 'therapist toddler.'

The basic concept is this: placing a one-year-old toddler with these highly disturbed children enabled them to go back to the point at which their opportunity for normal development was originally taken away, i.e., somewhere between six and nine months old. That is when they would have started to be a nuisance to the hospital staff, with the result that they were tied into their cots. In some ways they had become stuck at the developmental age of just under one year old. Introducing them to a toddler who was playing naturally as a one-year-old, enabled them to join him in his play, or at the very least mimic a type of activity with which they felt comfortable.

For example, the children liked interacting with each other while rolling around with the giant fluffy duck. That might be age-appropriate activity for Alex (our therapist toddler), but we would not normally expect to see a six-year-old (Virgil) or a ten-year-old (Nicolae) playing with cuddly toys for an extended period of time. However, these were children whose previous lives had been effectively shut down. They had not long been released from their captive state. It is my contention that the very natural behaviour of Ion triggered a memory in these older children which enabled them to play in a way that felt entirely natural to them. In effect they were able to re-start their play-based development.

In a second example, Alex climbed into a yellow rubbish bin, and Virgil started to play a game with him, involving an imaginary object. He pretended to receive something from Edit (the Romanian playworker) and then took it back to Alex in the box, who took it from him and put it in his lap. The yellow bin was real—everything else was in the children's imagination. At the time, our therapist toddler was around 15 months old, while Virgil was 6 years old. Given that Virgil had spent the previous five years tied in a cot, the quality of their 'symbolic play,' as Piaget (1951) would call it, is impressive. Again, my contention is that the very natural toddler behaviour of Alex sparked something in the mind of Virgil that enabled him to create an entirely novel game. Alongside numerous similar instances, this contributed to Virgil's rapid developmental recovery.[4]

We cannot know exactly what was going on in the complex minds of Virgil, Nicolae, Alex, and Liliana. The beauty of the playwork approach is that they were all free to explore their own thoughts and feelings in their own way. That essential truth was especially attractive to Brian. We were in strong agreement (and fascination) about the very substantial complexity of the different layers of play. Although he provided us with a generalised definition of play ("the potentiation of adaptive variability" - 1997, p.231), Brian was nevertheless clear that it is not possible to know what any specific moment of play means for the child who is playing—unless they tell us, and even then, it may only provide a momentary glimpse.

But what does this mean for playwork? My final thought is this:

For the watching adult, a child's play only provides a slightly open window to their world. As playworkers we are privileged when they sometimes allow us to peep through. In many ways, a child's play is like an impressionist painting—a representation of how they see reality. Playwork provides the canvas for children to produce an ever-changing masterpiece of their own reality.

Brian felt strongly that during play children constantly create and recreate a world of their own—a process he called, "learning to control their own little microcosm of the world" (Sutton-Smith 1992). That is what he found attractive about playwork—i.e., in its purest form the playwork approach seeks to provide environments that enable children to play as they wish.

NOTES

1. NB. The playwork approach is very different from that which is adopted by the US Playworks organization.
2. This reflection appeared previously in Brown (2014)
3. Harlow's methods would be considered completely unethical by today's standards.
4. These two examples are derived from video footage and reflective diaries kept by Sophie Webb at the time (all names have been changed).

REFERENCES

Brown, F. (2014) *Play and Playwork: 101 Stories of Children Playing.* Maidenhead: Open University Press
Brown, F. (2018) *Longfellow Lecture—Giving Children Hope: The Value of Therapeutic Play.* Sarah Lawrence College, New York. 12th April 2018
Brown, F., Long, A. and Wragg, M. (2018) Playwork: A Unique Way of Working with Children. In: Roopnarine, J. and Smith, P.K. (2018) *The Cambridge Handbook of Play: Developmental and Disciplinary Perspectives.* Cambridge University Press
Brown, F. & Webb, S. (2005) Children Without Play. *Journal of Education,* 35, Special Issue: Early Childhood Research in Developing Contexts, March 2005
Fisher, K. (2008) Playwork in the Early Years: Working in a Parallel Profession. In: Brown F. & Taylor C. *Foundations of Playwork.* Maidenhead: Open University Press
Pedersen, L. (2023) Playful Choreographies and Choreographies of Play: New Research in Dance and Play Studies. *American Journal of Play,* 15 (1) pp.60–81
Piaget, J. (1951) *Play, dreams and imitation in childhood.* London: Routledge and Kegan Paul
Suomi, S.J. & Harlow, H.F. (1971) Monkeys Without Play. In: Bruner, J. S., Jolly, A., & Sylva, K. (eds.) (1976) *Play: Its Role in Development and Evolution.* New York, Basic Books
Sutton-Smith, B. (1992) In: Channel 4 documentary: *Toying with the future.* London, Channel 4 Television

Sutton-Smith, B. (1997) *The Ambiguity of Play*. Cambridge, MA: Harvard University Press

Trevarthen, C. (2005) First things first: infants make good use of the sympathetic rhythm of imitation, without reason or language. In: *Journal of Child Psychotherapy*, 31 (1) pp.91–113

Webb, S. (2014) Therapeutic Playwork Project: Extracts from a Reflective Diary. In: Brown, F. (2014) *Play and Playwork: 101 Stories of Children Playing*. Maidenhead: Open University Press

Chapter 12

Brian Sutton-Smith

Notes and Snapshots

Jeffrey Goldstein

As a young teacher in Wellington, New Zealand, Brian wrote a series of children's books that reflected how children in New Zealand actually spoke and behaved on the playground, which was not always with tact or consideration. This landed him, and not for the last time, in hot water. He was always a mischievous academic and relished the role. Brian was the best friend of every bad boy and girl, a defender of children's culture. For example, he did not condemn play fighting or view it as aggression, but as a form of struggle for identity, power, and status within a set of self-imposed rules. As a result, he was sometimes a controversial figure.

I first met Brian at a humor symposium in 1976. A description of the symposium in *New Jersey Psychologist* (1977, vol. 27, no. 2, p. 17) noted that *'Dr. Brian Sutton-Smith gave astonishingly funny examples of pornographic stories composed by his young subjects.'* We became friends soon afterwards.

Brian was that rare colleague who shared my interests in and love of humor, play and sports, and their academic study. I was fortunate that Brian moved to the University of Pennsylvania in 1978 and we became near neighbors in the Philadelphia suburbs. We would visit occasionally or meet at the Penn faculty club, where he introduced me to interesting colleagues with whom I would later work. It was always rewarding to bounce ideas off him because they came back enhanced.

A lecture by Sutton-Smith was a dazzling, dizzying experience — exciting, and over before you could catch your breath, or before your cognitions could re-align. It seemed that he was talking mainly to himself, thinking aloud in his stream of consciousness way, and I was fortunate to be a witness. A typical lecture would include references to philosophy, biology and brain

Figure 12.1.   Brian all kitted out, 2010. *Courtesy of Jeffrey Goldstein.*

research, developmental and social psychology, anthropology and folklore, and it would be scattered with the often-obscene stories, games, rhymes, and jokes of the school children whom he studied. All in the service of a better understanding of children's play. Here is an example. It is a quote from a 1992 seminar, where Brian talked about the idea that play prepares children for the future.[1] He used as a springboard the recently introduced doll *My Bundle Baby* (Mattell) that appeared to be pregnant and could be used to simulate pregnancy. He examined media reports about the doll, which most often expressed alarm that *My Bundle Baby* would misinform young children about childbirth and serve as an incitement to pregnancy. The reports frequently quoted child development experts who confirmed the need for concern. Here is Brian's far-ranging assessment of the controversy.

What these antipathetical voices show us is how profound is the belief among some educators in the United States that child play is a specific preparation for adult development. All of these voices imply that what happens in play, down to the minute particulars of this doll, will have a great effect on the future of the players and of their country. . . .

As an aside, the European Judy doll, which has a belly that snaps off to reveal a baby, is said to have caused no such explosion of concern in Europe.

The historical forces that predispose us to think about play in causal terms is immense. These include millennial hopes of the Reformation. The Panglossian expectation of eighteenth-century rationalists that the physical sciences could be replicated by the social sciences and human progress ensured. The growth of various kinds of historicism, like those of Hegel or Marx, which assumed that humanity could conceptualize human history as progressive and predictable. . . . The growth of a science of childhood, which, following the metaphors of evolutionary theory, came to assume that childhood development occurred in predictable stages and . . . that it was also possible to find childrearing antecedents for later life outcomes. Although many of these beliefs, a great empire of optimism about predictable social progress, have largely gone down into the dust of secularism, holocausts, fascism and communism, the scientific production of bombs and pollution, as well as the empirical reality of the low-level scientific predictability of human behavior in general, the habit of thought still hangs on to maintain the illusion that such micro phenomena as Bundle Baby or Judy have detailed predictable consequences.

In 1993, Brian and a dozen other toy researchers gathered in Utrecht to form the International Toy Research Association (ITRA www.itratoyresearch.org). The 30th anniversary meeting of ITRA took place in August 2023 at the Strong National Museum of Play, in Rochester, NY. (www.museumofplay.org).

Brian's focus on how children play forced him to confront interactive toys and video games, which he did with his usual insight and verve. In November 2003, I moderated a discussion between Brian (via video link from Florida) and game designer Eric Zimmerman at the first conference of the Digital Games Research Association at the University of Utrecht, the Netherlands (www.digra.org). Prior to the conference, Eric, who had never met Brian, asked

SEARCH

112

Chapter 12

Figure 12.2. First meeting International Toy Research Association. Utrecht, The Netherlands, 1993. From left: Rachel Karniol, Stephen Kline, Gisela Wegener-Spohring, Hein Retter, Waltraut Hartmann, Jean-Pierre Rossie, Brian Sutton-Smith, Peter K. Smith, Kathleen Alfano, Gilles Brougére, Birgitta Almqvist, Anthony Pellegrini, Jeffrey Goldstein, Maria Bartels (admin.), Greta Fein, Jorn-Martin Steennold. *Courtesy of Jeffrey Goldstein.*

me what sort of questions he should pose. I said all he had to do was ask any question at all and Brian would be off and running, which is of course what happened. It was a fine introduction to games scholarship and introduced Brian and his ideas to a generation of game developers and researchers. As with most other toys and games, video games and interactive toys are about rapid adaptation to changing conditions, a vital skill for survival. But Brian was uncertain about the relative net benefit of digital games. While he recognizes the cognitive, perceptual, and social benefits of video games, at the same time he laments the move from self-directed outdoor play to indoor screen-based play. As video games developed into mass multiplayer games with real-time communication and millions of players, Brian became more optimistic about their promise to create communities and promote adaptive behaviors (Sutton-Smith, 2017).

Students and scholars around the world are grateful to Brian for his support of their research on play. Often there were few or no others around with a similar interest, and Brian proved an accessible, genial, helpful and supportive voice for play research. His unbridled enthusiasm for the topic sustained many students and convinced many examining committees that children's culture is a worthwhile subject for study. Students from Asia, Africa, Europe, North and South America have said that without Brian's supporting

Figure 12.3.   Brian and the Sutton-Smith children: Katherine (Moyer), Leslie (Blackman), Mary (Tucker), Emily (Lepard), Mark. *Courtesy of Jeffrey Goldstein.*

letter or encouraging words they would not have been able to conduct their play research.

Brian continued to play tennis and to write until infirmities prevented him from doing so. His life was not all fun and games. But despite life-altering events, including the loss of his wife Shirley and son Mark, he lived with joy. He was a model of how to age gracefully and seamlessly.

Dinner with Debbie Dorothy G J Ed & Sarah Claflin and Brian Sutton-Smith

Figure 12.4. Brian Sutton-Smith (right) with Deborah Thurber (left), Gerda Kuiper and Jeffrey Goldstein (center), and friends. 17 May 2005, Beacon Restaurant, New York City.

Figure 12.5 Brian Sutton-Smith, Gill Gray (British Toy & Hobby Association), Jeffrey Goldstein. London. October 1992. *Courtesy of Jeffrey Goldstein.*

Courtesy of Jeffrey Goldstein.

NOTES

1. In October 1992, there was a public forum on toys and play in London, where Brian was joined by Gilles Brougére, Dorothy Singer, Jerry Singer, Peter K. Smith, and other luminaries of play research. Their presentations were published in my book *Toys, Play, and Child Development*. The quote is from Brian's chapter, 'Does Play Prepare the Future?' pp.135–136.

REFERENCES

Goldstein, Jeffrey (ed) 1994 *Toys, Play, and Child Development.* Cambridge University Press.
Sutton-Smith, Brian 2017. *Play for Life: Play Theory and Play as Emotional Survival.* Rochester: The Strong. pp.182–195.

Chapter 13

My Hybrid Hundredth Birthday Celebration for Brian Sutton-Smith

Elizabeth Tucker

The hundredth birthday of our friend and colleague Brian Sutton-Smith is approaching, so I'm going to throw a party. As a scholar, friend, and all-around wonderful human being, Brian has enriched our lives enormously. I'll never forget his retirement party in Philadelphia, which his friends and family had planned. Each of us who came to the party received a toy! I still have mine, a tiny yellow truck. It hasn't been easy to have in-person parties since the COVID-19 pandemic began but Zoom and other online programs have given us alternate forms of celebration. As Fraser Brown reminds me, Brian always enjoyed finding new ways to look at things, so I hope he would approve of this hybrid approach.

Since a hundredth birthday is a momentous occasion, I'd like to write a poem in Brian's honor. I am not a talented poet, but an amazing new artificial intelligence program, ChatGPT (Chat Generative Pre-Trained Transformer), launched in November of 2022, offers poetry to anyone who can type a query into a text box. Here is the poem I received from ChatGPT when I typed "write a poem about New Zealand play scholar Brian Sutton-Smith":

> Oh, Brian Sutton-Smith, the play scholar grand,
> Your wisdom on play is cherished in this land.
> From New Zealand, your birthplace so fair,
> Your teachings on play have spread everywhere.
> Your love for play was clear to see,
> In all the books you wrote with glee.

The Ambiguity of Play, your classic tome,
Is a treasure for scholars and parents at home.
Your theories on play have opened our eyes,
To the wonder and joy it can bring to our lives.
You showed us that play is more than just fun,
It's how we learn, grow, and become.
You knew that play is vital for kids,
To develop skills that they will use in their midst.
The creativity, resilience, and imagination it brings,
Are just a few of the wonderful things.
Your work has touched hearts far and wide,
From educators to parents and kids who abide.
Your legacy on play is here to stay,
And will guide us on our path every day.
So, here's to you, Brian Sutton-Smith,
The play scholar who taught us to love and live.
Your insights and wisdom will never fade,
As we continue to explore the world of play.

What would Brian have thought of this poem? I like the poem myself, although it hints at the sinister possibility of computers taking control of our lives. Humans still control machines, and we can enjoy playing with chatbots until they start playing with us.

While planning Brian's hybrid celebration, I've been thinking about children's birthday party traditions in New Zealand, and the U.S.A. In New Zealand, birthday party guests clap once for each of the child's years, with one more clap added for good luck. There may be special foods, such as pineapple lumps and pavlovas. New Zealanders take birthday cakes very seriously. According to Jazmine Nixon, author of *The Great New Zealand Birthday Cake Book* (2016), a creative cake is essential for birthday happiness. Nixon's book offers a dizzying array of cakes that look like kiwis, sheep, and other New Zealand creatures. I don't have enough time to make one of those elaborate cakes for Brian, but I can order a cake and decorations online. Through the magically swift process of ordering from amazon.com, a cake and a decoration for its top will appear.

Besides a birthday cake, a special dinner is traditional in New Zealand and the United States. In many families the birthday child asks for a dinner of favorite foods. Since I don't know Brian's favorite foods, I have decided to make the birthday dinner that my mother always made for me and my sisters: a potato man with a hamburger body, a mashed potato head, celery arms, and carrot legs. This kind of dinner was a huge treat back in the 1950s. Instead of cooking hamburgers, I am cooking healthful organic turkey burgers. My husband has asked why this birthday dinner is a potato man, not a

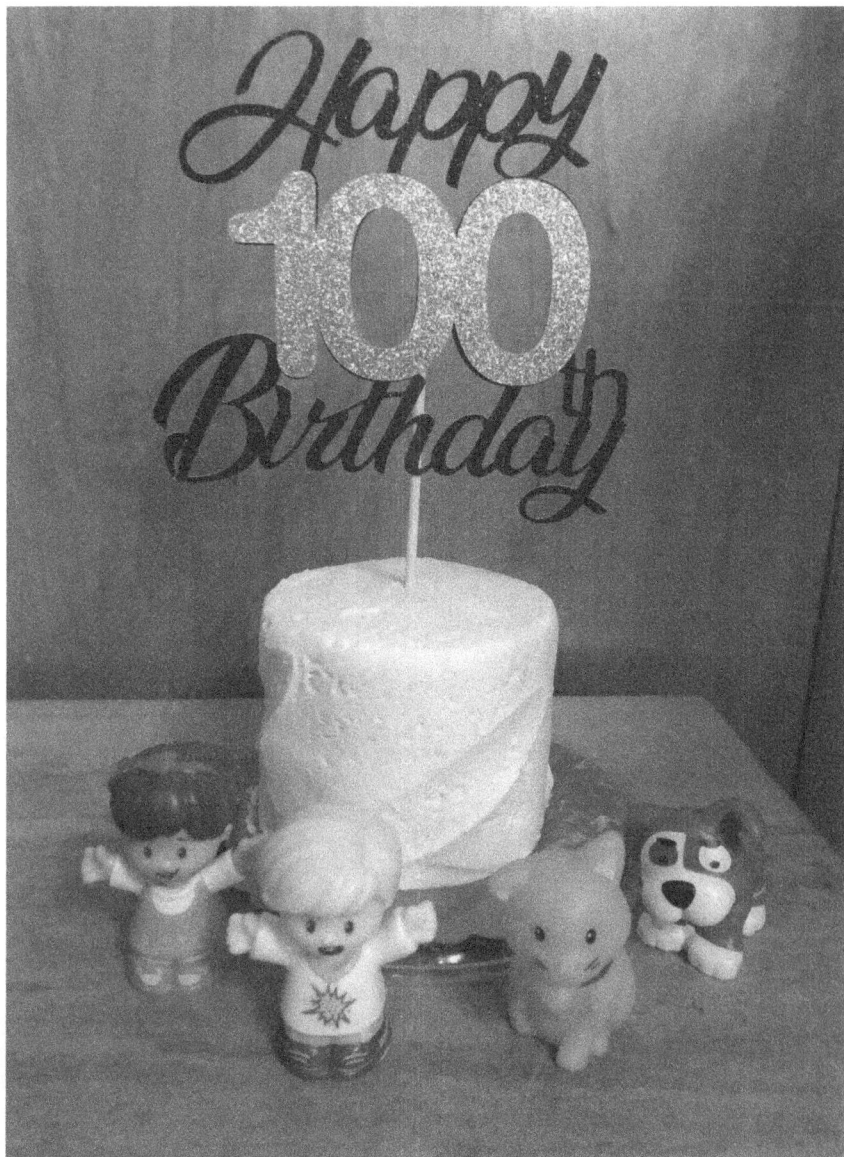

Figure 13.1.   Brian's 100th Birthday Cake. *Courtesy of Elizabeth Tucker.*

potato of a different gender. The only explanation I can give him is that men ruled in the 1950s; it never occurred to me when I was a kid to ask for a potato woman.

Staying with the potato theme, I've decided to buy a toy: Mr. Potato Head, a toy of the 1950s that is still available online. When I was a child, I

Figure 13.2. Brian's 100th Birthday Meal. *Courtesy of Elizabeth Tucker.*

watched my family's small black and white Motorola TV, listening in rapt wonder to a catchy advertising jingle: "It's Mr. Potato Head and his bucket of parts: buckets of fun for everyone!" Dying to get this marvelous toy, I asked my parents, and they got me one for my next birthday. I didn't know then that Mr. Potato Head had been inspired by a child poking sticks into a real potato to make it look like a face. Potato Head toys have had a long, lucrative career, morphing into potato-shaped plastic figures of different ages and genders; they have even advertised Lays potato chips on TV. Although "Mr." has been removed from the toy's official title, you can still see gendered versions of the

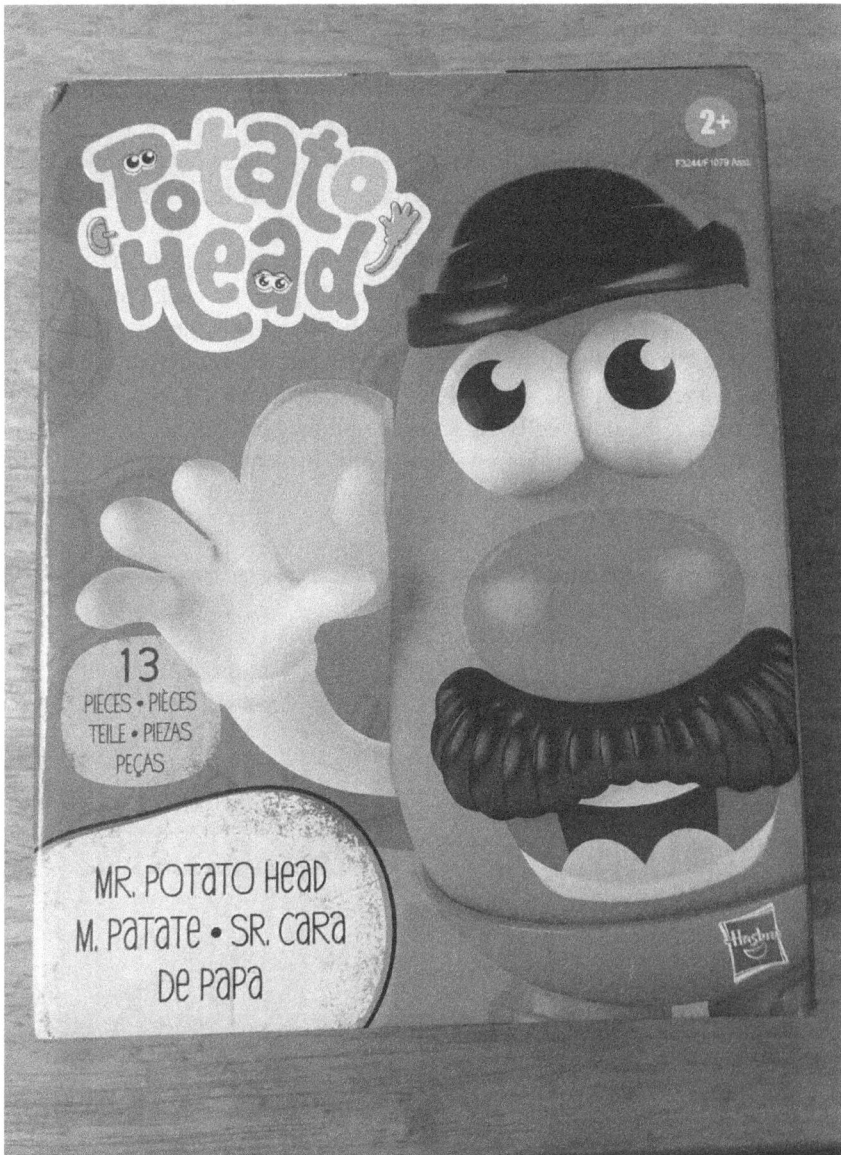

Figure 13.3. Mr. Potato Head, M.Patate, and Sr. Cara de Papa. *Courtesy of Elizabeth Tucker.*

toy's name in different languages on the front of the box: Mr. Potato Head, M. Patate, and Sr. Cara de Papa.

Who is coming to this party? Because of winter weather and COVID-19, my list of party guests is small: my husband Geof, our grandchild Daisy, our golden retriever Holly, and our cat Zorro. I have invited my friends in the happy hour group Folklore Thursday to wish Brian a happy birthday online in the evening. It's always great to see them, and their beautiful cats and dogs add to the happy hour's spirit. Since the spring of 2020, when the COVID-19 pandemic disrupted our daily routines, this group has met online regularly to chat, solve problems, and play games such as PowerPoint Roulette, in which all players present slides that they have never seen before. Folklore Thursday is a very playful group that rises to special occasions with gusto.

Now it's the morning after Brian's party. The in-person human guests loved their potato dinners, and the canine guest tried her best to cadge bites of turkey. The cat seemed indifferent to everything. Our granddaughter Daisy ran around the room practicing her newest word, 'watermelon," while playing with blocks and other toys. She will get the Potato Head toy as a gift for her second birthday. We enjoyed Brian's cake but didn't put candles on it for fear of fire risk from the paper "Happy Hundredth Birthday" decoration that had arrived from amazon.com just in time.

Figure 13.4.   Brian's 100th Birthday Party Attendees. *Courtesy of Elizabeth Tucker.*

In the happy hour after dinner, we talked about Brian's research. Kaitlyn Kinney, the group's convener, posted a link to an article about Brian in the chat box. Using Zoom's video filter feature, several of us put on funny hats, floral crowns, and fancy borders. Kaitlyn held up a toy horse wearing a party hat while Elinor Levy cuddled her beautiful orange cat. I held up the "Happy 100th Birthday" decoration that had been on Brian's cake earlier that day, and we took several screenshots.

Through artificial intelligence, Zoom, and Amazon.com, a playful, slightly outrageous celebration took place. Happy birthday, dear Brian, happy birthday to you!

REFERENCE

Nixon, W. (ed.) (2016) *The Great New Zealand Birthday Cake Book*. Auckland: PQ Blackwell Ltd.

Chapter 14

Incorporating Adult Play in Graduate Education

Inspired by Brian Sutton-Smith

Myae Han, Ekaterina Novikova, Stephanie Kuntz, Ariadni Kouzeli, Sharon Davis, Amy Santos, and Margo Harlan

It was 2002 when I first met Brian Sutton-Smith at The Association for the Study of Play (TASP) conference in Santa Fe, New Mexico. I was a doctoral student at Arizona State University researching play and literacy. My advisor, Jim Christie introduced me to Brian. Brian had a great sense of humor and was also serious. Despite only speaking briefly, I immediately sensed his quick wit, intelligence, and playful sense of humor. Although I cannot recall the exact topic of our conversation, I do remember the feeling of continuous laughter and seriousness. His keynote session was incredibly funny, and I was amazed to learn that academics can be fun. As an international student who immigrated from Korea, this was revolutionary, and I loved it. Brian inspired me to be a more playful scholar and teacher.

Brian's work on adult play was inspirational when I created a graduate course, *Play and Human Development*, at the University of Delaware. Originally, the course was from an early childhood educator's perspective and called *Play and Early education*. As I studied Brian's work and worked with graduate students struggling to understand child's play, I realized I needed to change the course significantly and incorporate a different method. My colleagues at the TASP and Brian have been my resources and inspiration for including adult play in my class.

As Brian advocated, the definition of play should extend to adulthood, and play is key to human development, not just child development. We should recognize its variations and see the play as a progress and tool for adapting to constantly changing worlds. This notion of play was a crucial point for me to extend my course content to adulthood and a lifespan perspective on studying play. I experimented various ways of how play unfolds with graduate students over time.

During the class, we explored a variety of play materials and various approaches, with the aim of discovering more about ourselves and how play can positively impact our well-being. Each student had a unique play personality, and I encouraged them to embrace their inner player by trying different types of play, such as Cat's Cradle, ball games, solitary play, cooperative play, constructive play, object play, brain teasers, improvisation, role playing, and board games. Through these playful experiences, we discovered new aspects of ourselves and strengthened our connection with others, all while having fun and learning the benefits of play.

Throughout the semester, students explored a range of play activities and then shared their thoughts and reflections on the experience. As part of this process, each student wrote a personal quote or reflection on the value of play. Below, you will find a collection of these quotes and reflections, including my own.

Myae Han

"Play is a gift of life."

A gift is something you receive from someone else on a special occasion, such as birthday or an anniversary. When you receive a gift, you feel happy and valued, as though you are a worthy person and life is worth living. For me, play has the same effect. A playful life is a gift that makes me feel alive and fulfilled. Whether it is a playful class, a playful writing experience, a playful meeting, or even a playful argument, these moments remind me of the joy of life that is worth living. How fortunate we are to have the ability to play! I want to encourage my students to embrace play in all aspects of their lives. Why not use the power of play whenever we can and wherever we are! In and outside of class, I strive to create an environment that is both fun and serious, where play and learning go hand in hand.

Ekaterina Novikova (2nd year doctoral student)

"Play is the fuel of human functioning."

Figure 14.1.   Celebration. *Courtesy of Myae Han.*

Everyone has their own play activity that invigorates them. While one person enjoys a loud celebration, the other will find joy in reading a book. Play unites and allows people to understand themselves better. For me, it seems that play is undervalued for its rejuvenating properties that both children and adults desperately need. Although not immediately evident, play serves as a means to socializing, learning, honing in on new skills, relaxing, and processing complex emotions.

It is important to realize that play does not stop when childhood ends. Adult play is fragile as it can be ruined by deeply rooted perfectionism. Just like children, adults have a necessity to play, and the feelings of guilt should not deprive them of benefits associated with play. Ultimately, finding time for both work and play creates a much needed harmony in a person's life

Stephanie Kuntz (2nd year doctoral student)

"Play is the experience of joy when doing a supposedly purposeless activity. To the individual, it has great purpose and meaning."

Play is a privilege we take for granted and underutilize. We overlook the capacity of play to promote healthy development. Play is a source of resilience and reprieve when one is faced with adversity. Play allows us to rebuild our joy when the world has torn it down. Even in the most dire of circumstances, play can bring joy and passion into our lives.

Play has brought me joy and built my resilience through the lifespan, from being a sick kid playing with dolls in bed, to playing with loose parts in graduate classes with my friends and colleagues. In all cases, play sparks a fire inside my soul that makes me feel like I can conquer any of the world's challenges that come my way, and have a great time doing it. I want to spread the joy that play brings to children and families. Play is an excellent resilience resource, and to have resilient children and adults, we need to allow space for play.

Ariadni Kouzeli (2nd year doctoral student)

"Play makes you feel creative, constructive, excited, relaxed; generally transforms quickly your negative mood into a positive one."

Do you often return from your work or your school having negative thoughts or do you need to take a break before continuing your work at home? Play is the solution. Find materials and resources that you can use your hands or the whole body in order to distress from things that made you feel bad during your day. Working in a crowded environment such as a classroom or a company where you have to face wolves' behaviors, alluding to aggressive behaviors of students or co-workers, play can alleviate the pain that this type of behavior causes and it can arouse excitement in a short period of time.

Sharon Davis (first year masters student)

"Play provides a canvas for painting inner joy, sharing creativity, and reflecting the depths of your imagination for all to see."

It is impossible to say the word *play* without getting a huge smile on my face. As an early childhood educator, I am surrounded by three- and four-year-old children fully immersed in play. Solitary, cooperative, parallel and fantasy are all forms of play. However, *free play* is the greatest of all gifts you can give children. Being able to step back and use my senses to absorb the sights and sounds of children fully engaged in play is both an honor and a privilege!

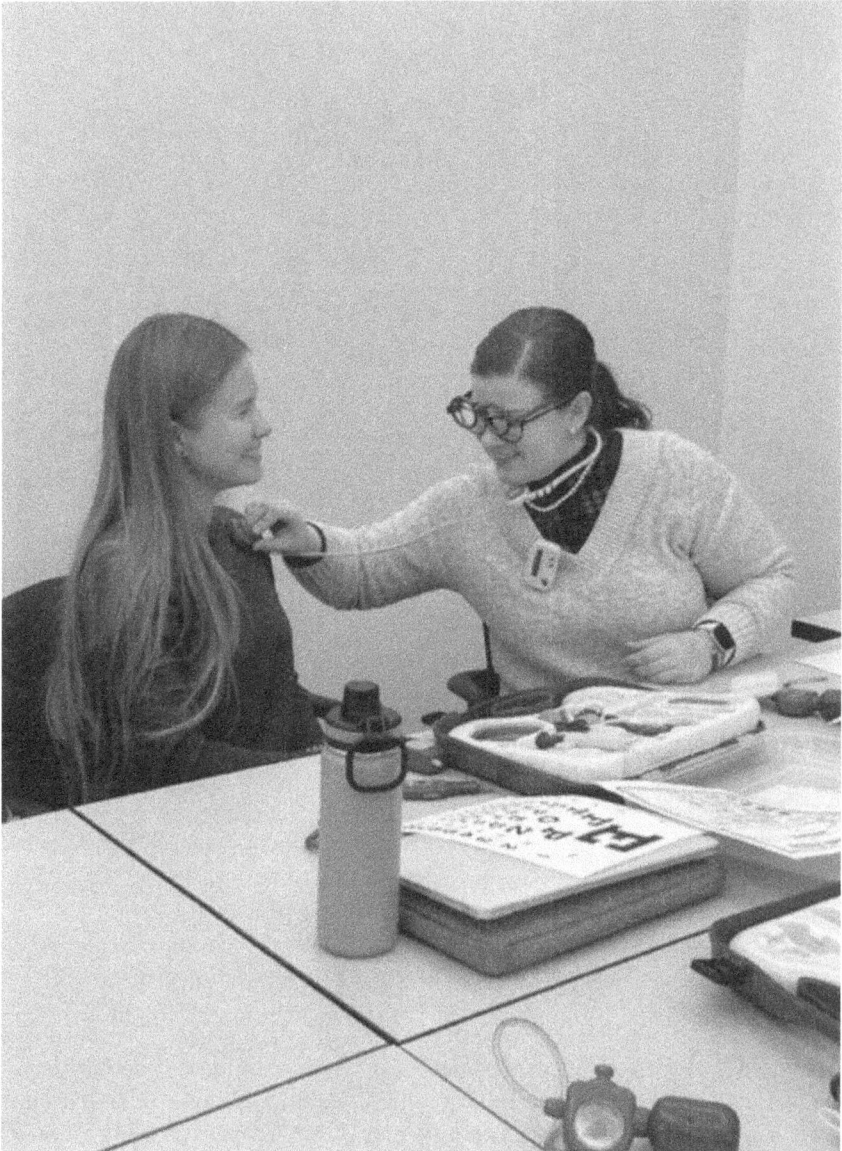

Figure 14.2.   Doctor Play. *Courtesy of Myae Han.*

Play is an activity essential for maintaining a positive outlook on life. The need for it does not end when you reach adulthood. Play is something essential for maintaining health and happiness throughout the lifespan. It was not until I began studying play in graduate school that I realized the extent to which activities that give me great joy are considered play. My love of

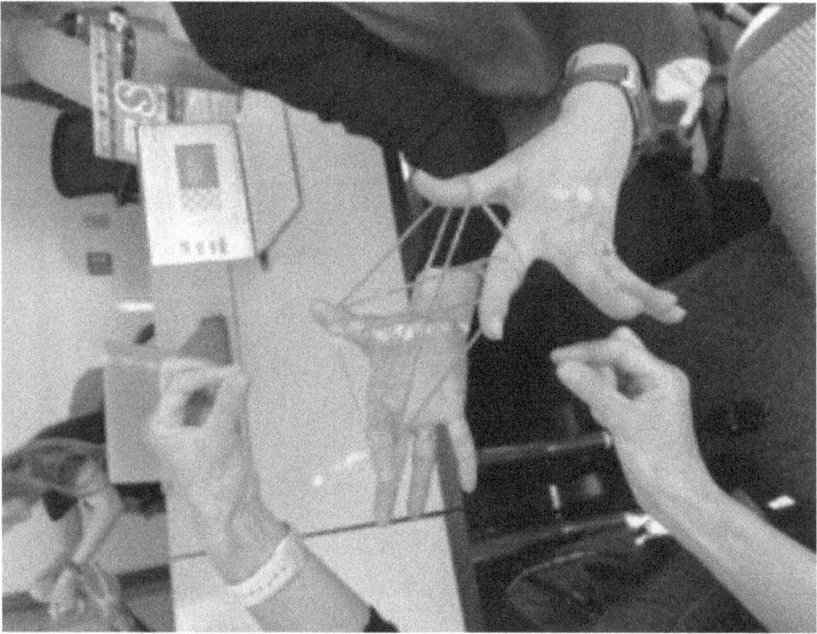

Figure 14.3. Cat's Cradle. *Courtesy of Myae Han.*

working with children, repurposing items to decorate spaces, curling up with good books and going camping are all parts of my *play personality.* These activities that define my love for play emerged when that little girl inside of me who loved playing with dolls, creating art and building tents, *grew up.*

Amy Santos (2nd year doctoral student)

> *"Through play, we can connect with our self and others, eliciting a range of emotions. Play can cost very little and provide so much. Play can be therapeutic, offering feelings of peace, joy, and belonging."*

In our class play experiences, I noticed a range of emotions. In solitary play, my feelings ranged from frustration at the exploration phase to satisfaction when immersed in play. As an adult, play is often not a priority for me. However, I am now realizing how important play can be and how it can act as a reset button when life needs a reset. Play helps us to know who we are, what we enjoy, what makes us unique. Play is timeless. It is an important part of our health and well-being at any stage of life. Learning about play research has impacted the way I approach my own life. I find myself encouraging my own children, parents, and self to enjoy play as a meaningful and important part of life; something we take for granted in children and often forget as adults.

Margo Harlan (1st year masters student)

"The time I feel my truest self."

Play is the only time I find myself releasing from daily stressors and the negatives from my life. As a person who overthinks, the world and my own thoughts constantly rush around me trying to swallow me into a whirlwind

Figure 14.4.   Play Workshop. *Courtesy of Myae Han.*

and play has become one of the few outlets that truly help me to *stop*. When I'm playing, I'm not worried with what paper I needed to write, what time I have to hit on my next race piece, or what I want my future to look like and how to do that. I feel content and calm. Play is a time when I find myself enjoying being in my own presence. When I'm playing, I feel like *me*.

Brian Sutton-Smith viewed play as a facilitator of children's creativity and a mechanism for adapting to the real world. After analyzing children's play in the form of jokes, which often came across as cruel and shocking, Sutton-Smith proposed that play is a protective factor against the uncertainties and injustices of reality. The play that occurs between parents and children not only strengthens the parent-child bond, but also allows for children's socialization, as evidenced in many cultures where parents prepare children for social integration through their teasing.

By engaging in play, both children and adults can escape to an imaginary world, and the joy and a sense of fulfillment gained in play can extend to real life. Sutton-Smith also emphasized the flexibility developed through play, which provides humans with an opportunity to practice a variety of skills to subsequently adapt to life as adults.

Thanks to Brian Sutton-Smith who made us realize the gift of play throughout the life-span. His theories and insights will continue to impact the lives of play researchers for a very long time.

Chapter 15

Inside the Brian Sutton-Smith Library and Archives of Play at The Strong

Jeremy K. Saucier

Brian Sutton-Smith searched for play, and its meaning, everywhere. In the first sentences of his 2008 article *Play Theory: A Personal Journey and New Thoughts,* the eminent play scholar noted that over the course of his career he thought "time and again I had at last discovered the meaning of play. But, somehow, it always turned out otherwise, somehow there always seemed other questions to ask, other lines of inquiry to follow, all arguing answers more promising than those I thought I had in hand" (p.80). This "ludic fishing expedition," as Sutton-Smith described it (p.80) started with his fictional account of his own rough and tumble childhood play in New Zealand; reached its peak with his 1997 book *The Ambiguity of Play,* in which he identified seven play "rhetorics," or ideologies (e.g.: play as fate, power, communal identity, frivolity, progress, imaginary, and self) adopted by members of particular groups or disciplines (p.8); and ultimately concluded with the posthumously published *Play for Life: Play Theory and Play as Emotional Survival* (2017).

In these and other published works, Sutton-Smith exhibited a deep curiosity, and most of all, a desire to widen our view of play. As Alice M. Meckley (2015) and Anna Beresin, Fraser Brown, and Michael M. Patte (2019) have so ably demonstrated, we can learn much from Sutton-Smith's published writings. But another way to continue the search for play's meaning is to explore Sutton-Smith's life and work more fully through his personal library, papers, and the multidisciplinary library named in his honor. In 2007, Sutton-Smith donated his entire research library of books, papers, and other play-related research to The Strong National Museum of Play. The museum designated its research library in his honor. In this essay, I do not attempt to closely analyze his personal library or papers. Instead, I offer a brief overview—with some illustrative examples—to these materials, and to the Brian Sutton-Smith Library and Archives of Play.

PERSONAL RESEARCH LIBRARY

Housed in The Strong's Brian Sutton-Smith Library and Archives of Play, Sutton-Smith's personal collection of research books is a veritable treasure trove for present and future play scholars and intellectual historians. Numbering nearly 2,200 unique titles, his research library includes major works on animal behavior, anthropology, child development, child psychology, cultural studies, early childhood education, folklore, games, history, humor, literary theory, mythology, neuroscience, philosophy, sociology, sports, toys, and video games. This collection illustrates his boundless curiosity and multidisciplinary approach to the study of play, while it also provides researchers with insight into how Sutton-Smith read these books—more than 1,400 of which include his annotations and marginalia.

Sutton-Smith often outlined or created his own additional index for pages related to play in the back of his books. Today, these indexes allow researchers to see not only how Sutton-Smith approached his study of these books, but also how he discovered useful connections to his work on play. For example, on the last page of his copy of the revised edition of primatologist Jane Goodall's *In the Shadow of Man*, Sutton-Smith created in pencil another index focused specifically on types of chimpanzee play. His index includes: page 29, "chasing, rotating, tug o war"; page 101, "tickling" and "chasing"; and page 156, "2–3 yrs spend most time playing." In the back of journalist Neal Gabler's *Life: The Movie*, Sutton-Smith captured notes such as page 10 "entertainment . . . as the primary value of U.S. life" and page 199 "Play as Consumption," "to change self, clothing, house, etc."

In some cases, Sutton-Smith's personal books are filled with notes and marginalia that provide windows into the time and his thinking when reading these books. His copy of historian Lynn Hunt's 1989 book *The New Cultural History*, an edited collection about the influence of anthropology and literary theory on a new generation of historians, is flush with circled phrases, underlined sentences, and notes that show him talking back to, and asking questions of, the text. On page 78 of Aletta Biersack's essay "Local Knowledge, Local History: Geertz and Beyond" in Hunt's collection, Sutton-Smith circles the sentence "The real is as imagined as the imaginary." Nearby this sentence, he writes "Play at Centre" (an observation he previously notes on page 11 of

Hunt's introduction), "This changes all interp of play to date," and "contrast w/ Schultz, Goffman, etc." Writing in the margins of the next page, he poses and answers the question "What is Geertz's kind of play? Playing cultural, diagnostic, clinician." He poses and answers the same question for Jacques Derrida, Erving Goffman, and Mikhail Bakhtin. Exploring the pages of Hunt's book provides the intellectual historian in particular with insight into a time when Sutton-Smith's research engaged with the work of anthropologists, sociologists, and theorists like Roland Barthes, Jacques Derrida, Michel Foucault, Clifford Geertz, and Erving Goffman.

Sutton-Smith's library also helps us better understand his movement from what he called the "cultural frame approach" to a more comprehensive theory of play that considered decades of research into brain science, emotions, and evolution. As Jay Mechling (2015) points out, Sutton-Smith found Antonio Damasio's 1994 book, *Descartes' Error* particularly useful to support his third play theory, or what he described as play as a coevolutionary multiplex of functions. Not surprisingly, Sutton-Smith's copy of *Descartes' Error* is heavily annotated. His notes in the back pages of the book illustrate him working through the concept of a duality of primary and secondary emotions (Figure 1).

Similarly, although "play" shows up only once in the index to John Morgan Allman's *Evolving Brains*, Sutton-Smith's hand-written index, which documents connections to play throughout the book, includes a note that on page 50, "play as like gene mutation." Looking closely at page 50 of *Evolving Brains*, we can see how Sutton-Smith begins working out the relationship between play and gene mutation. It's an idea he explores more fully in the third chapter of *Play for Life*, where drawing on Allman's work, he asserts that "the continued presence of the original genes allows the reflexive or reflective conflicts of a species to persist; but parallel to this, the presence of the novel, mutated gene instead allows, through its representations for the imitative and imaginary experimentation of new traits and behaviors, a process we have, in this case, come to call play" (Sutton-Smith, 2017, p. 80).

PROFESSIONAL AND PERSONAL PAPERS

Also housed at The Strong, Sutton-Smith's papers document seven decades of his play research, teaching, and writing. Assembled and organized from 45 bins of research papers, after processing, the collection amounted to 171 archival document boxes arranged into a series of professional papers and a series of personal papers.

His professional papers include:

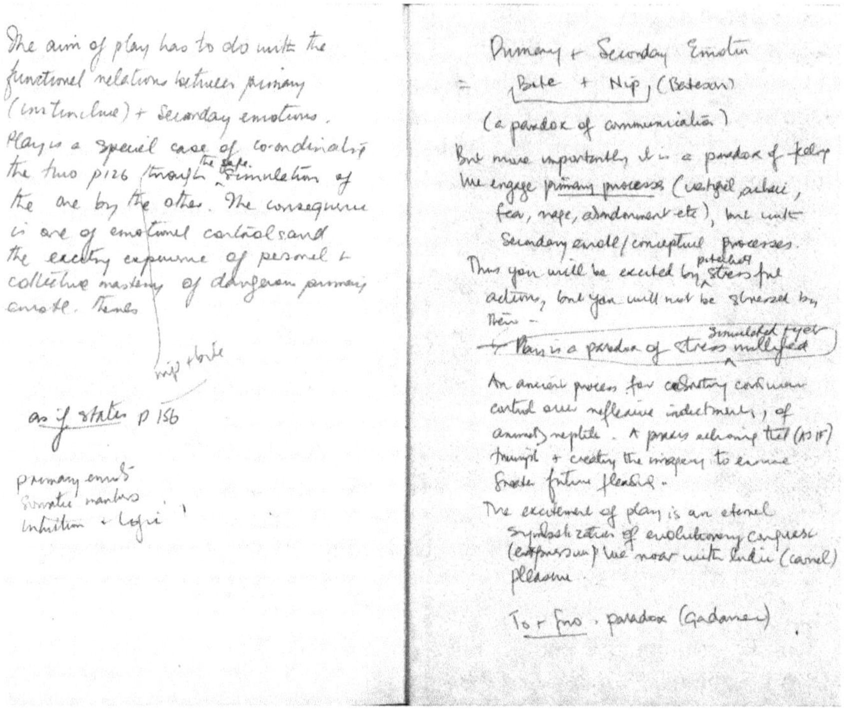

Figure 15.1. Sutton-Smith's notes in *Descartes' Error* on play and primary and secondary emotions. *Courtesy of The Strong, Rochester, NY.*

- Original manuscripts: These boxes contain text drafts of articles, article reviews, book chapters, book forewords, book reviews, conference papers, consultant reports, keynote speeches, prefaces, and presentations.
- Publications: These boxes house some of Sutton-Smith's many published articles, book chapters, book reviews, book forewords, and reports.
- PhD dissertation data and related materials: These boxes include original collected data, correspondence, manuscripts, news clippings, and notes.
- Research files and notes: These nearly 150 boxes contain all of Sutton-Smith's research files and notes, including audio cassettes, conference information, correspondence, draft text, floppy disks, lists, newspaper and magazine articles, notes and notebooks, organizational newsletters, photocopied reference materials, reviews of colleague's writings, and VHS cassettes.
- General correspondence: This box contains general correspondence files organized by date: 1951–1976, 1984–1996, 1997–1999, and 2001–2009 and no date.
- Publicity, diplomas, and awards: These boxes house bios, curriculum vitae, information on the 1983 TAASP roast of Sutton-Smith, lists of

honors, news clippings, professional diplomas, publicity materials related to his works, and recommendation letters.
• Materials related to his partnership with The Strong: This box includes correspondence and reference related to the *American Journal of Play* and National Toy Hall of Fame selection advisory committee; exhibit script reviews; and various agreements.

His personal papers include:

• Correspondence: This box contains personal correspondence files from the 1960s through the 2000s.
• Photographs: This box includes family photographs and photographs which were loose in Sutton-Smith's papers, including original photographs of his grandmother from the 1890s.
• Memorabilia: This box houses school childhood memorabilia and other personal ephemera, including school awards and certificates from the 1930s and 1940s and Sutton-Smith's passport.
• Family history: This box contains historical information and research on Sutton-Smith's father and genealogical research on his lineage.
• Manuscripts: These boxes house various draft manuscripts of fiction and/or nonfiction stories written by Sutton-Smith.
• Miscellaneous materials: These boxes include various documentation, including notebooks, hobby reference, and a diary from 1957.

But what might researchers expect to find in the hundreds of archival folders packed with documentation? I offer two brief examples of materials that help us learn more about Sutton-Smith's life and work.

In 1949, Sutton-Smith received funding to conduct doctoral research on play and games of New Zealand children. In addition to observational research, Sutton-Smith used newspapers and radio to ask New Zealanders to provide him with information about how they played. Over the course of three years, he collected data from hundreds of people who described their recollections in handwritten notes, or through interviews and a questionnaire. Sutton-Smith's papers from this period include examples of correspondence from New Zealanders, a book listing interview and report participants, his "New Zealand Children's Play and Games" questionnaires, notes, photographs of Māori schoolchildren, his dissertation, and a scrapbook of collected news clippings about the dissertation project. These materials not only potentially provide researchers with rich source material on play and games, but they also help document a formative period of Sutton-Smith's life as a scholar. As he later noted, members of his dissertation committee objected to his use of "racy children's rhymes and cruel jokes" in Sutton-Smith's dissertation

(Sutton-Smith, 2008, p.90). Although he resisted, he was forced to remove these and the episode revealed something essential about Sutton-Smith's work: children's play wasn't always "nice," and he wanted to document and understand the pleasant and not so pleasant aspects of it, regardless of how adult's imagined children should play.

Decades later, Sutton-Smith still explored new forms of play. Some of my favorite documentation from this collection comes in the form of a group of notes, printed artwork, and printed clothing related to Sutton-Smith playing and studying the 1996 computer games *Barbie Fashion Designer* and *Barbie Storymaker*. *Barbie Fashion Designer* allowed players to choose from a variety of themes, styles, patterns, and colors to design clothing for their own Barbie dolls. They could then turn these designs into real doll clothes by printing them on special paper-backed fabric through a home printer. *Barbie Fashion Designer* proved wildly popular with young girls, and Sutton-Smith's reflections on the game capture some of the reasons why. His notes contrast the difficulty of printing and assembling the real Barbie doll clothing and her unrealistic body proportions with the fun digital play that included "choosing outfits (You are the designer); modeling outfits (Prancing Around)." Judging from Sutton-Smith's notes, he thought the less popular *Barbie Storymaker*, which allowed players to craft their own animated stories, also lacked the depth of play afforded in *Barbie Fashion Designer*. As he observed, "This is playing with pieces of story"; "More of a scene director than a story maker"; and "More like directing a movie than being a novelist." Similarly, he asked, "Where are the story constructions," while adding a reference to see his 1981 book *The Folkstories of Children*.

Given that Sutton-Smith's wife Shirley's name appears on the printed artwork (Figure 2), it's likely that the two played the games together (or he observed her play), but either way, these materials illustrate how he never ignored any kind of play. Like a music producer always on the lookout for her next great act or some new experimental genre, Sutton-Smith was open to studying play in all its forms.

From these brief examples, it's easy to see the immense potential that Sutton-Smith's books and papers hold for researchers. But these books and documentation are also part of a much larger, multidisciplinary collection of materials related to the history of play.

THE BRIAN SUTTON-SMITH LIBRARY AND ARCHIVES OF PLAY AT THE STRONG

Located at The Strong National Museum of Play in Rochester, NY, the Brian Sutton-Smith Library and Archives of play is a multidisciplinary research

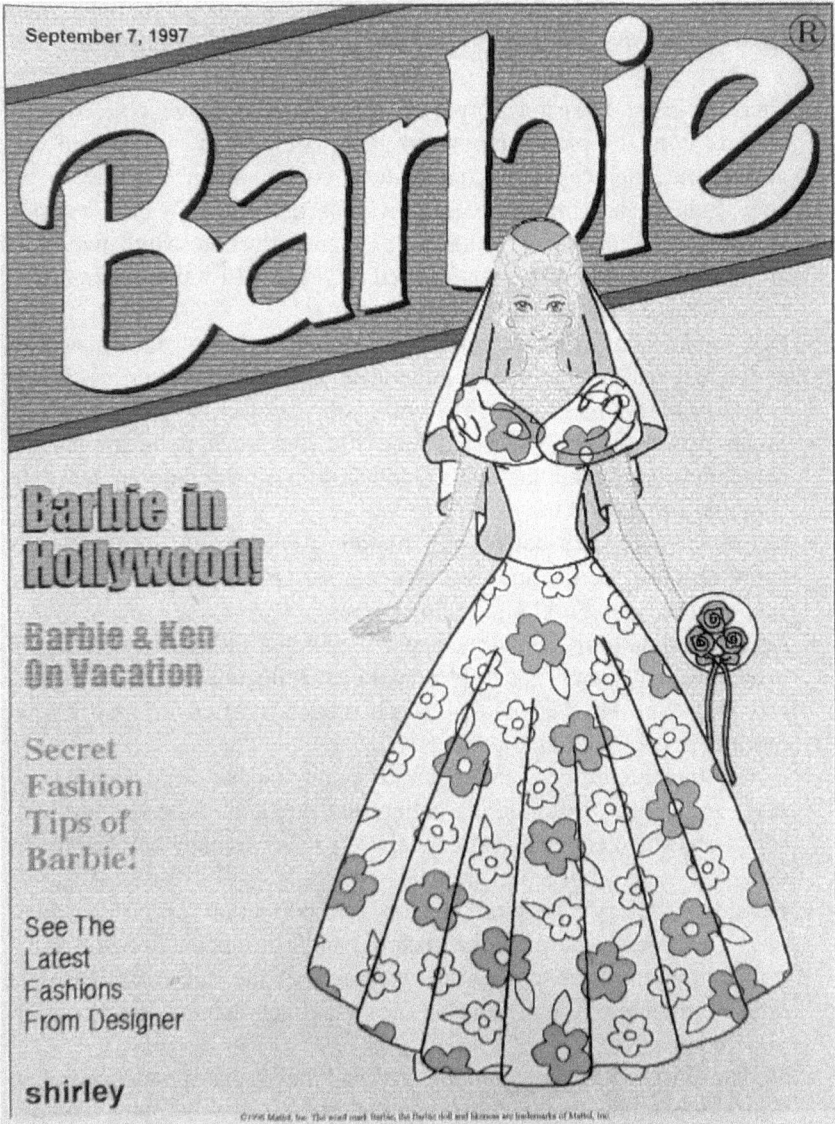

September 7, 1997

Barbie

Barbie in Hollywood!

Barbie & Ken On Vacation

Secret
Fashion
Tips of
Barbie!

See The
Latest
Fashions
From Designer

shirley

Figure 15.2. Printout of *Barbie Fashion Designer* dress design on faux magazine cover. September 7, 1997. *Courtesy of The Strong, Rochester, NY.*

depository devoted to the intellectual, social, and cultural history of play. The more than 230,000-volume research library and archives holds an unparalleled collection of primary and secondary sources, including scholarly works, professional journals, other periodicals, trade catalogs, children's books, comic books, manuscripts, personal papers, business records, and more.

In addition to housing the personal library and papers of its preeminent namesake, among the representative library and archival holdings are:

- Atari Coin-op Division corporate records: A massive collection of records from the pioneering video game company, including artwork, design and engineering documentation, correspondence, game source code, industry and market research, videos, and company newsletters.
- Doris Bergen papers: A grouping of manuscripts, research materials, and primary source materials created or recorded by the distinguished educational psychologist.
- Doll Oral History Project collection: A compilation of documentation, audiocassettes of oral history interviews, associated transcripts, photographs, and reports on this 1987 oral history project.
- Stuart Brown papers: An assemblage of manuscripts, publications, correspondence, research materials, and recordings from the founder of the National Institute of Play.
- Game Show History collection: A continuously growing collection of game scripts, specification documents, press kits, photographs, audiovisual materials, and oral history interviews.
- Lella Gandini Early Childhood and Children's Folklore collection: A grouping of research notes, presentations, reference materials, journal and magazine articles, and other documents created or used by the prominent early childhood educator.
- Gund, Inc. records: A collection of legal papers, financial ledgers, photographs, toy patterns, marketing and publicity materials, artwork, scrapbooks, and company history related to the company best known for its Teddy bears and stuffed animals.
- Gerald A. "Jerry" Lawson papers: A compilation of design documents, business records, court records, and other papers related to the trailblazing engineer who led development of the first cartridge-based home game console and founded the first Black-owned game development company.
- Vivian Gussin Paley papers and Vivian Paley Correspondence collection: Collections of papers consisting of articles, news clippings, conference and workshop items, as well as draft manuscripts, audio recordings, notes, and correspondence donated from other scholars related to the esteemed early childhood educator.
- *Playthings* magazine: The most complete run (1903 – 2010) of the once primary trade journal of the toy industry.
- Sid Sackson collection: An interlocking collection of dairies, correspondence, design documentation, and game prototypes from one of the most influential American board game designers.

- Carol Shaw papers: A compilation of game design documentation, notes, sketches, source code printouts, advertisements, and other ephemera relating to the career of the first widely recognized professional female video game designer and programmer.
- Dorothy and Jerome Singer papers: An assemblage of publications, research materials, correspondence, and consultation documentation and scripts related to the influential psychologists' work on television shows such as *Barney* and *Sesame Street.*
- The Association for the Study of Play records: A collection of documentation, including correspondence, memos, notes, minutes, membership forms, brochures, programs, financial records, publications, and audiocassettes of conferences from the Association for the Anthropological Study of Play (TAASP, 1973–1986) and the Association for the Study of Play (TASP, 1987-present).
- Will Wright collection: A grouping of notebooks related to the prominent game designer's work on *SimCity 2000* (1993), *SimCopter* (1996), *The Sims* (2000), and *Spore* (2008) video games.

The Strong cares for all these collections, assuring that these materials will be preserved and available to researchers long into the future. Alongside Sutton-Smith's published writings, his personal collection of books and papers, as well as the collections that have grown out of the Brian Sutton-Smith Library and Archives of Play, are among his most important legacies. Sutton-Smith searched for play everywhere. And his library, papers, and the library and archives named in his honor reflect that longing to discover play and its meaning. My mind spins thinking about all the possibilities that may come from future researchers consulting and studying these materials. What new insights might we glean from these materials over the next 100 years?

REFERENCES

Allman, John Morgan. 1999. *Evolving Brains*. New York: Scientific American Library.

Beresin, Anna, Brown, Fraser, Patte, Michael M. 2019. "Brian Sutton-Smith's Views on Play," in Peter K. Smith and Jaipaul L. Roopnarine, (eds.) *The Cambridge Handbook of Play: Developmental and Disciplinary Perspectives. New York: Cambridge University Press, pp.383–398.*

Biersack, Aletta. 1989. "Local Knowledge, Local History: Geertz and Beyond" in Lynn Hunt ed. *The New Cultural History*. Berkley, CA: University of California Press, pp.72–96.

Damasio, Antonio, R. 1994. *Descartes' Error: Emotion, Reason, and the Human Brain*. New York: Grosset/Putnam.

Gabler, Neal. 1998. *Life: The Movie—How Entertainment Conquered Reality*. New York: Alfred A. Knopf.

Goodall, Jane. 1988. *In the Shadow of Man—Revised Edition*. Boston, MA: Houghton Mifflin.

Hunt, Lynn. ed. 1989. *The New Cultural History*. Berkley, CA: University of California Press.

Mechling, Jay. 2015. "Sutton-Smith's Five Easy Pieces," *Children's Folklore Review* 37, pp.27–40.

Meckley, Alice M. 2015. "A Student's Guide for Understanding Play Through the Theories of Brian Sutton-Smith," in James E. Johnson, Scott G. Eberle, Thomas S. Henricks, and David Kuschner. eds. *The Handbook of the Study of Play, Volume II*. New York: Rowman & Littlefield, 393–405.

Sutton-Smith, Brian (1981). *The Folkstories of Children*. Philadelphia, PA: University of Pennsylvania Press.

Sutton-Smith, Brian (1997). *The Ambiguity of Play*. Cambridge, MA: Harvard University Press.

Sutton-Smith, Brian (2008). "Play Theory: A Personal Journey and New Thoughts," *American Journal of Play*, 1, pp.80–123.

Sutton-Smith, Brian (2017). *Play for Life: Play Theory and Play as Emotional Survival*. Rochester, NY: The Strong.

Chapter 16

A Sutton-Smith Mini Puzzle

Anna Beresin

One could say that Sutton-Smith himself was a puzzle. I think he would have enjoyed a puzzle in his honor. The answers will appear in Vol.13.3 of the *International Journal of Play*. If you peek at the answers, you lose bragging rights. Enjoy either way.

ACROSS

1. Speed of Brian's brain
2. A favorite number and dessert
3. A dialudic response to Brian's brain
4. With 1 down, his favorite childhood recipe for farts when consumed with raisins (True fun fact)
5. Scholars who surpassed him

DOWN

1. See 4 across
4. If we'd say pro, he'd say___
6. Half a kilometer in China
7. Peer rival in the UK
8. Homonym for Brian's favorite sports equipment

Appendix

Brief Reflections

A Celebratory Compilation

Fraser Brown

At the time of Brian's passing, I was privileged to be asked to collect the reflections of friends and colleagues. All manner of people from all walks of life expressed their sadness, as did most of the following contributors. However, we are keen for this book to be a celebration of Brian's impact on the World, and so the sad messages have been left out of this compilation.

* * *

Brian was our dear, playful, brilliant friend who inspired so many of us to delve into the realms of play in all of its manifestations. We hold a great memory of our shared time in Alicante. His books, memories, and great contributions on so many levels will never be lost. Let us share more about him, and always be glad for his inspiration, important contributions to TASP, and so much more. Three Cheers for Brian Sutton-Smith!—*Stevanne Auerbach*

The New York Times obituary made Dr. Sutton-Smith's passing real for me in a way I wasn't expecting. I never had the privilege of meeting him. However, his book *The Ambiguity of Play* continues to be a touch stone for me.—*Elise Belknap*

I agree with Dorothy that part of Brian's legacy is TASP!—*Doris Bergen*

Brian was a great colleague and supporter as I began working seriously on play. He was our leading play scholar.—*Gordon Burghardt*

Brian was always the top play scholar, in my humble opinion.—*Jim Christie*

Brian's legacy and scholarship will continue to influence play research for years to come. TASP members and the Strong Museum continue to honor and use his foundational theories in our research and practice.—*Lyn Cohen*

He lived a very full life, played well and deeply and with great heart. I was moved by how, along with his deep intellect and breadth of knowledge, he shared, from time to time, such tender caring for his students. And when it came to those wine and cheese socials for which TASP was founded (OK, there were other reasons), he was a fire-breathing delight to all. Party on, Brian. Cheers!—*Bernie De Koven*

I first heard of Brian Sutton-Smith when I was an undergraduate at Bowling Green University in Ohio. Though he had by then moved on to Columbia Teacher's College, the campus still reverberated with stories of the inspired teaching and impish good humor of this prolific young scholar, a dashing New Zealand import fully in tune with the sense of liberation and rebellion growing in America in the late 1960s.—*Scott Eberle*

I remember Brian with both affection and admiration, and know his significant work on play will live on. There are five English-language pioneers of the study of 20th century children's playlore—Dorothy Howard (USA), Iona and Peter Opie (UK), Ian Turner (Australia), and Brian Sutton-Smith (New Zealand and USA). This remarkably innovative quintet has been our guides and teachers—we are gratefully in their debt.—*June Factor*

An amazing man whose work has inspired me on so many levels for decades. While I was never lucky enough to meet him, hearing this news after spending the past few days at TASP with so many who were his friends seems fitting. In play, those degrees of separation evaporate. May we continue to delve into and explore his rich legacy.—*Stephanie Goloway*

To the sentiments that others have already shared, I will add my own feeling of profound gratitude.—*Dana Gross*

He was the most influential play scholar and we will never forget him.—*Myae Han*

A very useful, fruitful, 90 years happily, and well, spent. You can't ask for much more than that.—*Maggie Harris*

He was wonderful to be around - he thought seriously about play but he never took himself too seriously. I'm another one who had treasured conversations with him.—*Roger Hart*

Perhaps more than any other person, Brian legitimized the contemporary study of play and expanded its meanings. Because he opened those territories, the rest of us (including the rising generation of play scholars) are able to work more freely and productively. As great as his writings are, his more profound legacies may be the encouragement that he provided to so many others and his model of the ever-restless, rebellious spirit. May his life continue to resound.—*Tom Henricks*

I met Brian when I was a graduate student at which time he helped me find my way on the playground as he did for so many others. I know his life is celebrated every day on the streets, in the playground, and in those secret play spaces. He did and will continue to make the world a little more playful.—*Robyn Holmes*

Brian Sutton-Smith, play theorist extraordinaire and author of countless books and articles, perhaps most notably *The Ambiguity of Play.*—*Friends of IPA*

Brian both informed and inspired us. What a legacy he has left us all.—*Olga Jarrett*

A life well lived in inspiring and exposing others to the joy of play. With much gratitude.—*Audree Jones-Taylor*

His spirit will remain intact as a pillar of the TASP organization.—*Dorothy Justus-Sluss*

I feel so lucky to have rubbed elbows with so many great play researchers this weekend who knew, love, and respected him and are continuing his great legacy.—*Dana Keller*

Brian gave the single most brilliant conference presentation I've ever heard, on the ambiguities of play. I think it was at the joint TAASP-American Ethnological Society meetings in Baton Rouge in 1983. The contents have faded away after over 30 years, but not the wonder of his presentation. Brian didn't romanticize play—he knew it could be ugly, cruel, and nasty, like any other open aspect of the human condition.—*Rob Lavenda*

Brian will always remain the playmaster. We will miss his warm and caring presence, but continue to follow his playful spirit in our work and our life. What a privilege to know such a person!—*Alice Meckley*

I am a PE teacher at Katherine Delmar Burke's School. I have delved into play on many levels for many years. What a life and contribution to our world. I have a great last memory of having dinner with Brian the last time I saw him. We stayed up late and shared stories. I had a stomach ache from laughing so hard!—*Guthrie Morgan*

His writings along with Prof. Don Handelman inspired me to become an Anthropologist of Play, Games and Sports. I have read just about everything Brian Sutton-Smith has ever written. I only have one personal memory with him. Back in 2000 I sent him a draft of my doctorate for comments and suggestions. I sent it in March and asked if I could call him in July when I would be in the States to discuss it with him. (This was pre-Skype days for me). When I called him in July he answered the phone and immediately began discussing the doctorate in detail as if he had it right in front of him. I was so impressed. His comments and insights were a tremendous help.— *Avigail Morris*

His legacy will definitely live on. I was pleased to have explored his child-hood home of Island Bay New Zealand last year and climbed into the woods on the surrounding hills and the beautiful beaches that exist there and could better understand how early play in such a setting might inspire his work as an adult.—*Eva Nwokah*

His work, his wit, his support of so many play researchers — his legacy will resonate into future generations of play scholars and practitioners.— *Diane Parham*

In my courses here in Argentina, I'm still working with his books.—*Maria Regina Ofele*

Brian's work guided my teaching and research for more than three decades. He was so supportive of my work, and wrote beautiful and persuasive letters for me. I always think of him fondly, and with admiration. When I retired and moved, his were books that I kept. Let me join in remembrance.— *Stuart Reifel*

A lovely man.—*Stephen Rennie*

There will never be another Brian Sutton-Smith. He was there at the beginning when it was TAASP (The Association for the Anthropological Study of Play) and he has always been there for TASP as well as for anyone who has engaged with the study of play and especially for anyone who wants to play. I think Brian embodied play which is why he was such an amazing person and also researcher. I feel privileged to have known him and to have learned from his work and to have benefited from his support and encouragement. Brian and play are synonymous in my view. His playful presence in everything that he wrote and said will always be with us.—*Helen B Schwartzman*

It has been a privilege to have known Brian, who was such an original thinker and also engaging speaker. He will be greatly missed.—*Peter Smith*

I have several fond memories of both scholarly debates and late-night alcohol-fuelled story-tellings with Brian and his loyal Columbia students in the 1970s, which I hope I can share in a future TASP event.—*Phil Stevens*

And finally:

It's been said that we all die twice—once when we take our last breath and once when the last person speaks our name. Brian's work and the friendships he developed ensure that his name will be spoken for a very long time.—*David Kuschner*

Index

About the Contributors

Anna Beresin is professor of psychology and folklore in the Department of Critical Studies at the University of the Arts in Philadelphia, Pennsylvania. A student of Brian Sutton-Smith's, Anna was able to craft a double PhD in order to apprentice with Dr. Sutton-Smith in his two appointments at the University of Pennsylvania. Anna researches children's physical play, animal play, and the intersections of play and art. Her most recent book is *Play in a Covid Frame: Everyday Pandemic Creativity in a Time of Isolation*, coedited with Dr. Julia Bishop. An international collection, the book is free and available for download through Open Book Publishers. Her first book, "Recess Battles: Playing, Fighting, and Storytelling" won the Opie Award in Children's Folklore from the American Folklore Society. In 2024 she will be a Fulbright Scholar at the University of Sheffield in the United Kingdom. She coedits the *International Journal of Play* with her two illustrious colleagues, Dr. Fraser Brown and Dr. Michael Patte. Find her at: www.annaberesin.com

Fraser Brown is the first Professor of Playwork in the UK. On retirement he was awarded the title of Emeritus Professor. Previously he was Director of Studies for all postgraduate playwork research at Leeds Beckett University, and specialist link tutor for postgraduate play therapy courses run in conjunction with APAC. Before joining LBU he managed playwork projects in both the statutory and independent sectors. His research interests include the impact of deprivation on children's play behaviour, the assessment of play value in children's play spaces, and the role of play in Montessori education. He is known for his research into the therapeutic impact of playwork on a group of abandoned children in a Romanian paediatric hospital. He is a member of the All-Party Parliamentary Group for a Fit and Healthy Childhood, and he is Co-Editor of the *International Journal of Play*. He has either written or co-edited around seventy publications, including *Play in Hospitals* (2023); *Aspects of Playwork* (2018); *101 Stories of Children Playing* (2014); *Rethinking Children's Play* (2013); *Foundations of Playwork*

(2008); *Children Without Play* (2005); and *Play and Playwork: Theory and Practice* (2003).

Gordon M. Burghardt is Alumni Distinguished Service Professor (Emeritus) in the departments of Psychology and Ecology & Evolutionary Biology at the University of Tennessee. He received his S.B. and Ph.D. in Biopsychology from the University of Chicago. His research focus is on comparative studies of behavioral development and play encompassing: theoretical, historical, definitional, comparative, experimental, neuroscience, and modeling questions, published in numerous articles and chapters. He is on the editorial board of several journals including *Ethology, Journal of Comparative Psychology, American Journal of Play,* and the *International Journal of Play.* He is a past president of the Animal Behavior Society and the Society for Behavioral Neuroscience and Comparative Psychology (APA Div. 6) and is the latter society's 2020 recipient of the D. O. Hebb award for his scientific contributions. He has edited or co-edited several books, including the *APA Handbook of Comparative Psychology* (2017). He is author of *The Genesis of Animal Play: Testing the Limits* (MIT Press, 2005) and a co-editor of two 2023 special journal issues on play in the *International Journal of Play* and *Neuroscience and Biobehavioral Reviews.*

John Cash lives in Bloomington, Indiana. He holds a BFA from the Studio for Interrelated Media at Massachusetts College of Art and Design, and a PhD from the Folklore and Ethnomusicology Institute at Indiana University. He has been a living history interpreter at several museums, he wrote his dissertation on Civil War reenacting, and he has published on the interactions of performance and historical commemorations. He has been a student and performer of commedia dell'arte since 2000. His latest book (2018) is a hand-made collaborative work of process art, resulting in a manuscript using only historical processes and techniques from the Middle Ages.

Jay Cross, author of "40 Brilliant Comedies—Easily Played, Updated, Commedia dell'Arte Scenarios From Flaminio Scala's 1611 Collection 'il Teatro delle Favole Rappresentative'," lives in Eastern Massachusetts and has been performing and studying this improvised Sixteenth Century theater form since 1985. In his other forms of play, he enjoys his family, studies astronomy (both modern and historic), makes short comic movies, pursues his family origins through genealogy, and numerous other amusements. His next book of historic Commedia dell'Arte scenarios is due out in February of 2024.

Sharon Davis is a graduate student at the University of Delaware working towards a Master of Science Degree in Human Development and Family

Sciences with a concentration in Early Childhood Development and Inclusive Education. She also works as an early childhood educator teaching preschool at the University of Delaware Early Learning Center. Sharon's primary interest is studying the role of play in diverse early childhood settings.

June Factor is widely known as a leading figure in the study and distribution of children's folklore, and a major collector and analyst of the playlore and language of Australian children's verbal and physical play. Much of her research is housed in the Australian Children's Folklore Collection, held in the Melbourne Museum. She is an Honorary Senior Fellow in the University of Melbourne's School of Historical & Philosophical Studies and an Honorary Associate of Museum Victoria.

Jeffrey Goldstein has been at Utrecht University (The Netherlands) since 1992 where he is currently research associate at the Institute for Cultural Inquiry. Among his 16 books are *Toys, Games and Media* (with David Buckingham and Gilles Brougére, Taylor and Francis, 2004), The *Handbook of Computer Game Studies* (with Joost Raessens, MIT Press, 2005); *Toys, Play and Child Development* (Cambridge University Press, 1994); and *Why We Watch: The Attractions of Violent Entertainment* (Oxford University Press, 1998). He is a Fellow of the American Psychological Association and the Association for Psychological Science. Goldstein served on committees of the Netherlands Institute for the Classification of Audiovisual Media (www.kijkwijzer), and PEGI, the Pan-European Video Games Rating Board (www.pegi.info). He is a recipient of the BRIO Prize (Sweden) for research 'for the benefit and development of children and young people.' He is co-founder with Brian Sutton-Smith and Jorn Steenhold of the International Toy Research Association (www.itratoyresearch.org).

Sylwyn Guilbaud, PhD, is an independent researcher, artist, and home educating mother of three. She qualified as a Playworker in 1997 and returned to Leeds Beckett University to complete one of the first doctorates in the sector in 2011. She lives by the sea, where she loves to wander and wonder, drawing inspiration for part of her current play-advocacy—the creation of small stitched magical beings in support of the playing relationship between children and the elements.

Myae Han, PhD is a professor in the Department of Human Development and Family Sciences at the University of Delaware, a past president of The Association for the Study of Play (TASP) and Early Education and Child Development SIG at the American Educational Research Association. She is a coeditor of Play & Culture Studies V. 15 and V. 16, Play and Curriculum,

Play and Literacy. Her research includes a play-based intervention, early language and literacy development, professional development.

Margo Harlan is a D1 rower and senior at the University of Delaware, studying to get her bachelor's degree in early childhood and special education while concurrently working toward her Master's Degree in Early Childhood Development and Inclusive Education. Her focus is on children receiving educational equity, especially in the preschool and early elementary years.

James E. Johnson is a Professor of Early Childhood Education at The Pennsylvania State University and is a Past President of The Association for the Study of Play (TASP). He is the current Series Editor of *Play and Culture Studies* and is on the editorial board of the *International Journal of Play*.

Ariadni Kouzeli is a PhD student in Human Development and Family Sciences at the University of Delaware. She received her bachelor's degree in educational sciences and early childhood education from the University of Patras in Greece and her master's degree in educational studies with Applications in Information Communication (ICT) from the University of the Aegean also in Greece. Ariadni currently works as a graduate research assistant studying nature-based early childhood curriculum and instruction. Her research interests include teacher education, curriculum, nature education and multicultural education.

Stephanie Kuntz is a Ph.D. student in Human Development and Family Sciences at the University of Delaware. Stephanie earned a Master of Science Degree in Child Development and a Bachelor of Science in Child Development with a Minor in Business Administration and Emphasis in Infant and Toddler Development from the University of La Verne. Previously, she worked at NAEYC accredited Child Development Centers and as an Early Intervention Home Visitor for children 0–3 with developmental delays or at high risk of developing them and their families.

Ana Marjanovic-Shane is an Independent Scholar, Professor of Education, and deputy editor-in-chief of *Dialogic Pedagogy: An International Online Journal* (https://dpj.pitt.edu). She received a doctorate from the University of Pennsylvania, USA. Her main professional interests and research are focused on the following issues: dialogic meaning-making and creativity in human development and education, democratic and dialogic education from and for the agency, play and its humanizing potentials in education, dialogic relationships in educational events, play, drama, and art in education, teaching as conceptual art, etc. Her articles in English and Serbian were published in various journals (e.g., *Mind, Culture, Activity Journal, Learning, Culture and Social Interaction, Dialogic Pedagogy Journal*) and as book chapters in books on play and education. Her recent publications include Marjanovic-Shane, A. (2023). Dialogic pedagogy in democratically run schools: Introduction. *Dialogic Pedagogy: An International Online Journal, 11*(2), A12-A20.; Marjanovic-Shane, A. (2023). Four person-ideas in a soul-searching internally persuasive discourse. *Dialogic Pedagogy: An International Online Journal, 11*(2), A198-A216; and Matusov, E., A. Marjanovic-Shane & M. Gradovski, (2019). *Dialogic pedagogy and polyphonic research art: Bakhtin by and for educators*, Palgrave Macmillan. Ana lives and works in the USA.

Peter McDonald is assistant professor of design, informal, and creative education in the department of Curriculum & Instruction at the University of Wisconsin-Madison. His work explores historical transformations in playfulness, and the problems of interpreting play.

Jay Mechling is Professor Emeritus of American Studies at the University of California, Davis. He is a Fellow of the Americana Folklore Society and recipient of the Davis Prize, the highest honor at UC Davis recognizing outstanding teaching and research accomplishments. He is a Past President of both The Association for the Study of Play and the Western States Folklore Society, editing that society's journal, *Western Folklore*, for five years. He is the author of three books on masculinity, including *On My Honor: Boy Scouts and the Making of American* Youth (Chicago, 2001), and over one hundred forty journal articles, book chapters, and encyclopedia articles. He is co-editor, with Brian Sutton-Smith, of *Children's Folklore: A Source Book* (1995).

Ekaterina Novikova is a PhD student in Human Development and Family Sciences at the University of Delaware. Her research interests include language and literacy development, nature-based education, and immigrant families with young children.

Michael M. Patte is Professor of Early Childhood Education and coordinator of the Child Life Specialist and Playwork certificate/minor programs at Commonwealth University of Pennsylvania. Dr. Patte is a *Distinguished Fulbright Scholar*, Past President of *The Association for the Study of Play*, and Co-Editor of the *International Journal of Play*. He has authored, edited, and co-edited several books including *Play and Social Justice: Equity, Advocacy, and Opportunity* (2023), *Handbook of International Perspectives on Early Childhood Education* (2018), *Play and Culture Studies Volume*

13: Celebrating 40 Years of Play Research—Reflecting on Our Past, Exploring the Present, and Playing into the Future (2017), *Developing Mindful Home, School, and Community Relations* (2016), *International Perspectives on Children's Play* (2015), and *Rethinking Children's Play* (2013).

Amy Santos is a PhD student and research assistant in the School of Education at the University of Delaware. Her research interests are shaped by her experiences as a first-grade teacher, teacher educator, parent, curriculum director, and reading specialist. She seeks to understand how children's literature, literacy, pedagogy, and play can make learning a more joyful, meaningful, and equitable experience for children, teachers, and parents.

Jeremy K. Saucier is Assistant Vice President for Interpretation and Electronic Games & Editor of the *American Journal of Play* at The Strong National Museum of Play in Rochester, NY. Trained in cultural, intellectual, and political history, he has developed or curated many exhibits on the history and importance of play. He is also the author or coauthor of several published works, including *A History of Video Games in 64 Objects* (2018).

Helen B. Schwartzman (Professor Emerita of Anthropology, Northwestern University) is a psychological anthropologist who specializes in the study of childhood development and play and the anthropology of work and organizations. As an Americanist, she is drawn to the study of everyday activities that have been neglected by researchers and taken for granted by participants. This has led to studies examining how children construct play worlds for themselves, the role of meetings in organizations and communities and storytelling in work settings. Her publications include *Transformations: The Anthropology of Children's Play (*1978), which was the first comprehensive examination of the literature on children's play in anthropology; *Play and Culture* (1980, Editor), *The Meeting: Gatherings in Organizations and Communities* (1989), *Ethnography in Organizations* (1993) and *Children and Anthropology: Perspectives for the 21st Century* (2001, Editor).

Elizabeth Tucker is a Distinguished Service Professor of English at Binghamton University, specializes in children's and adolescents' folklore, folklore of the supernatural, and legends. Her books include *Campus Legends: A Handbook* (2005), *Haunted Halls: Ghostlore of American College Campuses* (2007), *Children's Folklore: A Handbook* (2008), *Haunted Southern Tier (*2011) and *New York State Folklife Reader: Diverse Voices*, co-edited with Ellen McHale (2013). With Lynne S. McNeill, she is co-author of *Legend Trips: A Contemporary Legend Handbook* (2018). She has edited *Children's Folklore Review* and served as president of the

International Society for Contemporary Legend Research and the Children's Folklore Section of the American Folklore Society; she is also a Fellow of the American Folklore Society. For several years she has written a column on play for the *International Journal of Play*. She loves to play and go on legend trips.

www.ingramcontent.com/pod-product-compliance
Lightning Source LLC
Chambersburg PA
CBHW031136270326
41929CB00011B/1650